Comme Çi Comme Ça

Jottings from Normandy

by Vivienne M. Barker

First published worldwide 2014

Text copyright © Vivienne M. Barker 2014
All rights reserved

The author asserts the moral right to be identified as the author of the work

No part of this publication may be reproduced, stored in a retrieval system or transmitted in any form or by any means, electronic, mechanical, photocopying, recording or otherwise without the prior permission of the author

vivienne.barker@gmail.com

Introduction

Throughout my teaching career, I was involved in 'twinning' exchanges between schools in England and France. When my husband, Eric, retired at the youthful age of fifty-one, we decided to up sticks and move to France as our big adventure. We wanted to really live the adventure, not simply spend holidays there, so Normandy, with its temperate climate and accessibility to England hit the spot. After all, France and the French are all there, undiluted, from the moment you step off the ferry – no need to penetrate into the middle of nowhere, or *La France Perdue* as the French themselves call it. The French in Normandy are every bit as French as the people in, for example, the Limousin. You don't experience a sort of Franglais mixture of language and lifestyle the nearer you are to England.

During my subsequent fifteen years of living in Normandy I taught English to French people who needed to speak English for their work; from widget-making factory managers to hotel staff; solicitors to business people. I made friends in my village and my Englishness proved to be a passport into all sectors of society; whether it be the couple in the manor house with a 'de' preceding their surname; well-to-do *Parisiens* in their Normandy holiday homes; the local farmers or the mayor.

Teaching English was not only a marvellous opportunity to get to know people I would otherwise not have, but the very nature of the subject means that once the essential structures of the language are laid down, we had to talk about *something*. After all, English is only the medium not the message. The students were of all ages and from varying backgrounds too. I found them very honest when expressing their opinions – not given to want to impress the others – or me. They were less able to laugh at their own idiosyncrasies than we are, I think – although quite able to laugh at ours. They thought our rituals about Christmas-card sending were hilarious. I hope that we, too were honest and fair to our compatriots.

One couple became especially dear to me. Odile was French and very entrenched in French upper-middle class mores and her husband was a retired English airline pilot. After thirty years in England they had come back to Odile's homeland to enjoy their retirement in the countryside. Odile was a fabulous source of information about the French – from strict cooking (and eating) instructions to fashion tips such as wearing only transparent or *Hermès* red nail varnish.

So I was privileged to be close enough to French people that I could indulge in discussing our different outlooks on life. They were certainly as interested in learning from us about our way of life, as I was in them. So when I started to write a regular column for the magazine Northern Life, I thought it was going to be a sort of diary of my life, but it soon became clear from remarks from my readers that they enjoyed reading about the French and what they are really like. I struggled not to generalise about the French as I know we don't like it when they say we are all well-disciplined since we queue obediently at bus-stops, or accuse us of eating very badly, but after a couple of years I gave in to the temptation, when I realised that some generalisations could be seen in so many instances, that they are worth mentioning. I hope that the generalisations I make are not too exaggerated. Of course there are exceptions to every rule and not all French people behave or have the opinions I have attributed to them. However, there were certainly enough of the examples I mention to capture my attention and the exceptions merely proved the rule. So what follows are articles written on different topics that interested me because our two outlooks on them are different. I thought they might interest the magazine's readers at the time and I hope they may interest you now.

Acknowledgements

It was thanks to my husband, Eric, that the idea first arose to gather together these articles, first published in the *Northern Life* magazine. The design of this book was supervised by Michael, my computer-buff son and I have been enormously encouraged by all my friends. A special thank you to Patty, my friend and writing mentor who has given an enormous amount of her time reading and advising on my writing in general. Always in my thoughts is Odile, my French friend, who first piqued the notion of the differences between our two peoples, which were the subject of great conversations over lots of dinners, *bien-arrosés* and who has sadly passed away.

Contents

1. Bienvenue En Normandie 1
2. Climate Change 5
3. Service With A Smile 9
4. Our Heroes 13
5. Etiquette 19
6. Holier Than Thou? 25
7. The Proof Of The Pudding 29
8. Home Sweet Home 37
9. Education, Education, Education 45
10. Two Parties 51
11. Little Things Mean A Lot 59
12. Food For Thought 67
13. A Visit To Marseille 75
14. Mind Your Language 83
15. La Crise Économique 91
16. Pets Or Pests 99
17. Ken's War 107
18. To Your Very Good Health 117
19. Driving You Mad 125
20. Ce N'est Pas Le Cricket 133
21. Women's Stuff 139
22. The River Dives 145
23. Farmer's Delight 151
24. Noel, Noel 157

Bienvenue En Normandie
December 2006 / January 2007

We lit the first log fire in the last week of October this year, so we are hoping the wood we just bought will see us through till the end of February. Summer started late – my tomato plants in the vegetable plot were set back by frost in May – but lasted long into October, when we were still having lunch on the *terrasse*.

Eric and I were both teachers of French in Lancashire, had always taken our family holidays in France and had great memories of twinning experiences with school pupils so when Eric was lucky enough to be offered early retirement when the Polytechnic he lectured at became part of a university, it didn't seem so illogical to move to France. After all, the youngest of the children was at university and it seemed time for our own adventure.

We wanted to live in the countryside as do most of us townies. We eliminated the Dordogne (too many English there already) and the South in general (too hot in Summer if you want to do more than lounge around a pool all the time – and what if you can't afford the pool?), the same for the centre of France which in addition has very cold Winters, Alsace (too Germanic) and the Alps (too claustrophobic in the valleys, and we are not skiers). So where to choose?

On the last coffee stop before the ferry home in 1990, we idly looked at a few faded black and white posters of houses for sale. We were in a town called Verneuil in Lower

Normandy. There were charming half-timbered cottages and larger houses at prices not seen in the UK since the seventies and by the condition of the photos, they were not flying of the shelves. All the way home on the ferry and on the drive north from Portsmouth we continued to daydream. We realised that with a teacher's pension coming to Eric within the next six months, we could live the dream.

So that's why we are in Normandy and I'm looking out over the view in the picture. When Winter evenings keep us inside and we have piled the apple-wood and got a good fire going, and when we switch the television over from the local news and weather, to Granada TV, it still gives me a jolt to see an advertisement for a Blackpool attraction or a car sales centre in Burnley. It's like electricity jumping an abyss, joining two worlds. That particular car sales centre is just a couple of streets away from where I was born and grew up. I keep looking round the edges of that T.V. ad for signs of the railway sidings which dominated my childhood; the nocturnal shunting which punctuated my dreams, the embankments we sledged down in the snow and rolled down on the dry summer grass. I imagine the station with its own coal fire in the wooden-benched waiting-room.

It is strange how France is – well, so French, even near the coast. I mean, you might think, with the channel only separating things English from things French by some twenty miles between Dover and Calais, that there would be a gradual changeover, a no man's land, where English culture and language were still commonplace along the French coast. But no; as soon as you step off the boat, the French are there at their pavement restaurants. You see customers sliding oysters (Ouistreham where the ferry docks outside Caen, means 'oyster village') down their throats, mopping up the juice with chunks of bread that they tear apart with their fingers, looking nonchalant and stylish with their jerseys (from the Isle of Jersey) thrown over their shoulders and knotted by the sleeves at the front. The waiters briskly place and clear dishes without a trace of subservience but with manners as if to the manor born.

In my diary, I'll be describing our lives here for you, and trying to put my finger on those differences between the two nations that have intrigued me (and I hope, you) all my life.

Oops, time to throw another log on the fire. À bientôt.

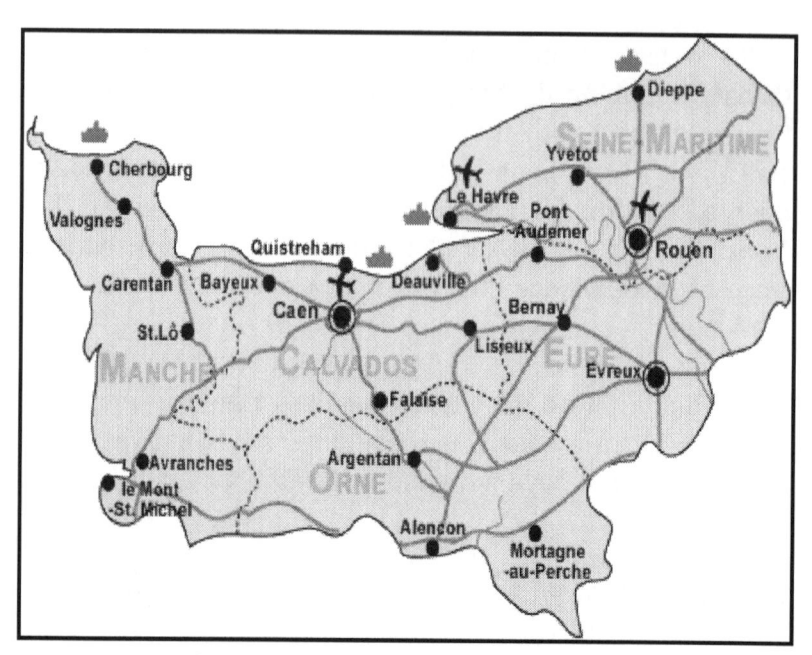

The Calvados département (county)

Saint Aubin sur Algot from our house

Climate Change
February / March 2007

We have lived in the Pays d'Auge for almost five years now, and although it is only around three hundred miles due south of East Lancashire, the climate is quite different. It is much drier here. It is several degrees warmer for most of the year, although probably a few degrees colder in the depths of winter. If last winter was anything to go by, this one will drag on a good while yet, so keeping warm is a priority at this time of year. And yet, we were still having lunch outside at the beginning of November.

We have opted for an electricity regime here called Tempo. We have electric central heating, so our consumption is high and we can save money with this regime. The standing charge is much lower as are the units of electricity used. However, on 22 occasions between November and March, EDF (the energy provider) warn us by way of an alert in the back kitchen that the following day will be a 'red' day. The war-time spirit then takes over. The washing machine is put on to do a last wash, the central heating is switched off from 6am the following morning and two gas heaters are wheeled out from the cloakroom and positioned in the kitchen and the garden-room where we are most of the day. Extra layers of clothing are worn, the dishwasher is not used, nor the iron. In the evening the two gas heaters are wheeled through to the living room and we light the fire in the chimney. The wood for the fire is neatly stacked behind the house, against the hedge. We buy it at the rate of four *stères* twice a year. A *stère* is one cubic metre and a local woodman delivers it. We all muck in and help to unload and stack it. In fact, after a few years here, we have realised that the stacks of wood lining the hedges of the properties are an outer sign of riches here in Normandy. The longer the pile, the richer the owner is. A far cry from a tiny bag of sticks you buy from a petrol station in the UK.

It's quite fun really - for a day or two, making do with the minimum of electricity. The EDF can decree up to 5 red days consecutively and then it's less fun as the hot water runs out. We are careful only to invite people at the weekend during this season because there is never a red day then. This system saves us quite a chunk of money over the year and helps French industry when the national grid is under strain on high-demand cold days.

Today is a red day. We have done a two hour stint on a gruelling job in the garden, lit the fire and we are now sipping Benedictine as I wait for the muse to get in contact. Benedictine is really a *digestif* for drinking with coffee at the end of the meal, but it's heart-warming on a day like today.

The first time I visited the Benedictine abbey at Fécamp, about two hours north of here, I got the surprise of my life to see 'Burnley' writ large on the wall display showing places where Benedictine is exported throughout the world. Yes, Burnley is the town (outside of France) which consumes most Benedictine in the whole world, and this is because the soldiers from the Lancashire Fusiliers got a taste for the stuff when they were stationed nearby during the First World War. My brother tells me that you can even pin-point the establishment in Burnley where most Benedictine is drunk (it is known as 'Benny and hot') to the miners' club on Plumb Street. My brother also tells me that there is a regular who drinks a bottle of Benedictine a day, but obviously he shall remain nameless.

The on-going outside jobs at this time of year are hedge-clearing and garden fires. We are fortunate in that it's really only the bottom hedge and the trees lining the top boundary that need attention because one side boundary is a neighbour's responsibility and the other is planted with conifers which don't need cutting as there is no neighbour on the north-east side. These conifers form a great wind-barrier and are a long way from the house and so they don't impede the sunlight. Still, there are some 200 yards to do as the land in total is 2.5 acres or 1 hectare.

This job is called the *élagage*. It's not hedge-trimming with a trimmer but a slow, labour-intensive process with saw, loppers, rope and secateurs. It's dragging out brambles, sawing down branches and clearing ivy and other parasitic growths on both sides of the hedge. All this has then to be dragged to two or three sites where later, it has to be burnt. If you neglect the hedge and branches risk falling on the telephone or electricity wires, the relevant body will write to you and give you notice to remove the offending branches or they will do it and charge you for it.

Some days, our neighbour, Erik comes out to see how it's going. He is encouraging us in what we are doing as taking off six to eight feet from the height of the hedge gives his house half an hour more daylight. Also he can use some of the bigger branches as fuel for his oven. Just opposite our gate is Erik's rustic *boulangerie*.

All his bread is organic, hand-kneaded and shaped, and baked in a wood-fired oven. We may not have shops in our tiny village but we do have our bakery. The bakery is cunningly twice-named with plays on the words for 'bread', 'pals' and 'ecology'. The home-painted wooden board announces *Boulangerie Les Copains* (The Pals' Bakery) on the way down the lane and *Boulangerie L'Eco-pain* (The Eco-bakery) on the way up. Say both titles out loud and you will hear that they sound the same. Erik doesn't make *baguettes*. He makes different sorts of country-style loaves with organic flour. He also does *brioches* and even pizzas. If he is off taking his bread to market, you just go in and take what you want from a basket on the stone-flagged floor and leave your money on the table.

Erik helps us with his chain saw to chop down the really big trees. He likes to show us – *les rosbifs* - how it's really done. Yes, the French call us by the name of what we supposedly eat – roast beef – just as we call the French 'the Frogs' because they supposedly eat frogs. This is not normally done within hearing though.

The evening is closing in already. We are warm from the work, the fire and the liqueur, and it feels good. I pull off a chunk of warm, crusty bread and think about my grandmother who worked in an Oddie's bakery shop for years. Only ten more red days to go.

Service With A Smile
April / May 2007

I was very flattered last summer when my daughter-in-law asked me to be her mentor. She was going to open a gift shop in the North Yorkshire town of Skipton and had a clear idea of her philosophies behind it all. Now it appears she has really tuned into the zeitgeist of the times with her shop in a little cobbled courtyard. She buys from local artists, her products use only recycled materials and if she buys from abroad it is under the fair-trade rules. So, as her mentor, I have had hardly any input at all except to suggest she adopt the French attitude to gift-wrapping.

One Christmas, about three years ago, I bought a fairly expensive present in a prestigious Preston department store. 'Would I like it gift-wrapped?' the assistant asked. I was delighted to see this small but wonderful service, which has been in operation in France for generations, being adopted in England at last. I was less delighted to be told to go up to the administration floor, where I had to pay £3 for the service and come back in an hour to collect the parcel. Here in France you are always asked if a gift-like purchase is *pour offrir* any time of year and the assistant will whip it into a crisp package with ribbon twirls and stickers in a trice. Right in front of you. Any other people waiting to be served will not be at all put out as they expect the same attention when it is their turn. Does it matter how little you are spending? To put this to the test, I went into a chocolate shop yesterday and asked for just one chocolate. True enough, the assistant didn't actually ask if it was to be given as a present but she did ask *'C'est pour vous, madame*?' and when I said it was for my husband, she beamed and shaved off a sliver of stylish paper from the roll attached to the counter and proceeded to create a mini work of art. Her pleasure in doing so was evident.

Gifts are an important part of life in France and need a little thought. When invited to a meal in a French home, it is not done to take a bottle of wine as we would do back home. If you did, you would be implying that your host cannot provide for you adequately – something like turning up with the meat for the meal in England. An exception to this rule would be if your wine was specially bought direct from the vineyard which only you apparently know about. Last month a couple came to supper with us and brought some home-made bottles of cider. In the same way, you can take food provided it is a little exceptional or something which has a 'story' to it – you bought it from a wonderful little shop you know, or it's a jar of preserves you have made yourself.

Flowers, as well as chocolates are the most usual gifts. Every tiny village, however down-at-heel, will have a florist. Flowers are not cheap but they are bought much more often than in England. You see husbands going home from work with flowers and they don't appear soppy about it either. Flowers are brought to take to *grand-mère*'s house for Sunday lunch, and here in the countryside that is what families do on a Sunday, go to have lunch at grandma's. If you haven't got a *grand-mère*, you go to a restaurant.

The patisserie is as hallowed as the chocolate shop and the florist's. This is because, although French women are generally very good cooks who have kept the family traditions of cooking handed down from mother to daughter, they tend to concentrate their efforts on the entrée and the main course. By the time they get to the pudding, they are all cooked out and for weekday meals with the family, there is simply fruit or yoghurt on offer. If visitors are invited to a meal the French housewife is very likely to buy the dessert at the patisserie. There is no shame attached to this practice. It is not considered cheating to buy the dessert. It will be a sumptuous affair and quite costly. Also there will be a 'story'. It will be from the best *pâtissier* in the area for this speciality. Once, at a meal in a far-flung suburb of Paris, the wife presented a sorbet which her husband had been sent to buy, that very afternoon, all the way into the centre of Paris. Such was the reputation of the ice-cream maker.

Any old *pâtissier* will have *religieuses* (so called because they look like a nun in her habit), *divorcés* (split choux-pastries) and meringues as big and as lumpy as my handbag. These last are my personal favourite sugar-fix. They are usually piled up on top of the counter but you rarely see anyone eating one. Not surprising really, but I wish people wouldn't always say 'You're not really going to eat all that are you?' as I struggle to get my mouth around one. A *pâtissier* worth his icing-sugar will have his own specialities. My favourite *pâtissier* in Lisieux makes a creation called *Sainte Thérèse* after the nun who made the town an international place of pilgrimage in the catholic world. This creation even comes with its own certificate explaining what the different components symbolise.

As for the philosophies behind the shops here, I can vouch they are all for local produce – it's just a way of life. They haven't had to re-invent farmers' markets here. All markets are and ever have been farmers'. Recycling is spoken less of, but the man who looks after the village tip on a Saturday sorts your stuff out into piles and you just know which piles he has found uses for. And fair trade probably means looking after your own in France, that is to say, 'buy French because everyone knows French is best'. That is why you see only a few bottles of token new-world wine in the supermarket and the odd cheddar cheese from outside the French borders. But most importantly in selling, presentation is everything. That's my top tip for my daughter-in-law.

Our Heroes
June / July 2007

Lower Normandy was liberated by the English in 1944, and soldiers from the Lancashire and Yorkshire regiments played an important part in it. The anniversary of the landings on the beaches and the subsequent liberation of towns and villages hereabouts is celebrated and honoured each and every year. The grand occasions, as for instance in 2004, the 60th anniversary saw various Heads of State assembled at Arromanches, Courseulles and Omaha. On these big occasions, French national and regional governments show unstinting generosity and a sense of the majestic which raises a ceremony to unexpected heights.

Back in 1994, the 50th anniversary, we were here too, at a whole day's celebrations by the hill at Montormel where the Polish soldiers plugged the famous Falaise Pocket and enabled the other allied troops to surround and defeat the Germans in what became the beginning of the German retreat from France.

On that occasion, in 1994, thousands of people gathered for picnics, religious ceremonies, wartime music and to see hundreds of re-enactment enthusiasts in their uniforms and army vehicles from the Second World War. After a glorious day milling in the crowds, we thought we had overstayed our welcome as we were preparing to go home about 10pm. But we were told it wasn't over yet. So we followed everyone else and gathered in front of a gigantic screen erected there in the valley under the hill.

We were overwhelmed, as darkness fell and the sounds of Beethoven's 5th came crashing along the valley, a silent film was shown on the screen of the whole of the D-day landings and the ensuing struggle up to the battle of the Falaise Pocket – people fleeing, dead horses and abandoned vehicles in the lanes, bombed homes and churches as the tenacious allies ground their way forward, the Poles holding their position on the hill even though they sustained huge losses. Above the screen, to the accompaniment of the reverberating music, was a magnificent display of fireworks that streaked and bejewelled the sky.

All this was entirely free, provided by the state. The French have a highly-developed sense of civic duty. And it's not only the landmark occasions that matter. Every year, each little commune will have its ceremony to remember a particular occasion from the war. All around us there are living memories of those times. Sixty years later you can still see stickers on the windows of cafés and restaurants announcing 'Welcome to our Liberators'.

I am sitting at our living-room window looking out at the building, which until the 1980s was the village school. The grim granite stone implanted in the village green was simply the half-mile marker in my early morning jog, until I realised it was a memorial; it took me weeks longer to notice that the Edmond Robert I thought it mentioned, was not Edmond but Edmone – a feminine name. Underneath, the sparse inscription reads:

Teacher at Saint Aubin sur Algot
From 1937-1942
Resistant arrested in her class
Deported to Germany
Died for France

I did some research and talked to our mayor and the retired village teacher. Our present mayor was a little boy in Edmone Robert's class at the time, although he was at home, sick, on the day she was arrested. The teacher who came to the village in the fifties and taught at the school until it closed in the eighties told me how she herself, had discovered a letter in the attic from her predecessor to the authorities about ration-tickets for the children's shoes, because some of them were not attending school because they had no shoes. There were also unusually placed locks in the schoolhouse where Edmone had concealed other resistance workers who had been involved with blowing up railway lines.

When the German Special Police marched into her classroom in 1941, she slipped some incriminating papers into a pupil's satchel. The pupil's father happened to work with the mayor, who was a staunch *Pétainiste* and Edmone's fate was sealed. After some months at the prison in Caen, she was tried and deported first to Lubeck in Eastern Germany, then to Jauer, south of Berlin. There, she was put to work in a Siemens factory making winding equipment for delayed-action bombs, but she soon contracted tuberculosis.

She was part of the long march of abandoned prisoners who were making their way to France as the Germans retreated, and so many died en route that it became known as the 'death march'. Edmone herself was picked up by the allies and driven in an ambulance towards the border. She died a few kilometres before reaching France. Her friend did not record her death until they reached Strasbourg, on French soil. She is commemorated each year, with hundreds of others, on the 'Day of the *Déportés*'.

There are many such stories, some grandly heroic, some quite trivial but moving and some amusing. A nearby *manoir* at Rusmenil, was bought for a song in the nineties because it had been a local German headquarters and had never been lived in since the war. No local French people wanted to live there.

An English student of mine, who works in a factory in Falaise, told me that his father was ten at the time of the allied bombings before D-Day. His village school was bombed and he never went to school again after that. I suppose, as a farmer's lad, there were other skills more important than reading and writing.

Our friend, Gerard de Forceville, was only ten when he, his mother and father and his brothers and sisters, were forced to flee their chateau at Bavent, near Ranville, (the first town in France to be liberated) when the fighting became intense after D-Day. They had to bicycle all the way to relatives in Lisieux carrying whatever they could. The journey took two days because they had to keep diving into the ditches to avoid air raids. The family chateau is still there but the family have not lived there since.

We were having supper with Gerard and his wife, when another guest, Alain, who was fourteen in 1944, told us how his family were living near Amfreville and had taken to sleeping and walking outside during one night a week since about March 1944 because air-raids made it unsafe to sleep inside a building. On the night of 5th June, outside their house, he and his mother were amazed to meet foreigners with blackened faces who were moving people along saying, 'Quickly, quickly!' His mother was astonished and in her broken English said to one of them, 'But where have you come from?' The English parachutist pointed upwards and replied, 'We've come from the sky!'

Another student, whose family have lived for generations at Bures-sur-Dives, near Ranville, told me how they have a ceremony every year on the evening of 5th June. Bures-sur-Dives had two bridges over the river, one for pedestrians and vehicles, and one for the railway. Soldiers of the parachute division which landed first near Ranville, had as their mission, to destroy all bridges between the river Orne at Caen and the river Dives to the East. In Bures, at the limit of the landing zone, Madame Vocant, a lady farmer, was out early to bring in her cows for milking from across the bridge. She was astonished to see soldiers, who turned out to be English parachutists, preparing to destroy the bridges. She begged the major to hang on until she could bring her cows across. Gallantly, the major did so. The war had to wait for the cows and every year until her recent death Madame Vocant was at the ceremony to thank the Major and the English veterans.

I wondered who those veterans were and can't find any personal memoirs of Bures-sur-Dives on the internet so far that provide a link. However, on the Army's official website, in 'A Short History of the Queen's Lancashire Regiment' I found that the 13th (Lancashire) Battalion Parachute regiment was the first parachute battalion in Normandy. On a French history site, I found the 13th Parachute Battalion and the 12th Yorkshire referred to again in Normandy. Their mission, according to this document was to secure Ranville, which was the first town to be liberated in France (Pegasus Bridge is just next to Ranville) and to secure the approaches to Ranville from the East.

Now, my student from Bures-sur-Dives tells me that the parachutists who were in Bures, had come from Ranville. If so, then Madame Vocant may well have been thanking our Lancashire and Yorkshire lads for delaying the war until the cows came home.

Incidentally in 1066 the sea flowed further inland at Dives-sur-Mer and the river at Bures was wider and deeper. Here William the Conqueror gathered his fleet ready to embark on a risky venture across the channel. It seems war is no newcomer to this region.

Saint Aubin sur Algot's schoolteacher and resistance worker, Edmone Robert

5 Etiquette
August / September 2007

There will still be individual shops in villages and small towns in England where customers say 'Good morning' to everyone in the queue for pies or pressed meat I'm sure, but the incomer to country life in France is struck by just how much good manners like that example permeate everyday life.

Every morning, in every office and factory in France, workers shake hands with all their immediate colleagues before logging on or getting down to work. 'What? Even people who argued the day before?' I ask.
'Of course' is the reply.
'Why not wipe the slate clean and start each day afresh?' I cannot argue with that. It seems such a civilised and positive way to begin the working day.

In France people greet each other properly whenever they meet. If you are merely acquaintances using *vous* to mean 'you', a handshake is required. If you are friends and use *tu* to mean 'you', four kisses are exchanged, alternatively, on each cheek. This varies a little from region to region but everybody knows the rules of the game – unlike us, the English.

We English are less sure of ourselves socially. We have adopted the kissing routine sometimes but not others. This can result in bizarre scenarios such as two couples meeting by chance in a shopping centre say, when they are delighted to see each other and exchange pleasantries but don't shake hands or kiss. However, the same couple might meet at one of their homes that very same evening for supper and there will be kisses and handshakes all round.

Should the French forget their manners on holiday, they will be reminded how to behave. In the seaside resort of Cabourg this year, there are notice boards as you leave the beach announcing, oh so daintily, that although you may be in swimwear on the beach, in town you should be appropriately dressed. Can you imagine this notice board in Brighton or Blackpool nowadays? In fact, in the seaside resorts along the Normandy coast, you see nothing but well-behaved families with children, or older couples on benches. It might be something to do with the amenities. There are no amusement arcades. There is no loud music. There are simply beaches, with children's supervised play clubs and lifeguards. There are restaurants on the promenade and some shops, but it's all low-key and rather gentile. You meet men in panama hats and, of course, everyone you pass greets you with a *bonjour*.

I find my Englishness difficult to shake off on some social occasions and sometimes it's misunderstood. The week before our village midsummer feast and bonfire, we had a committee meeting to discuss the arrangements. I arrived at the appointed time (8.30pm) and sat discreetly on the second row (mustn't be pushy), notepad and pencil at the ready. It took half an hour for the ten people on the committee all to come into the room, shake hands or kiss everyone else, be seated, ask me to move up a row and make sure everyone else was seated cordially. Then the Ricard, whisky, Calvados and a selection of mixers appeared from baskets and boxes brought by the ladies who had thought of everything including the ice-cubes. Another half-hour was spent asking what everyone would like to drink and ceremoniously pouring said drinks. Everyone proclaimed, *'Sante!'* Then they added 'chin-chin' for my benefit (didn't chin-chin go out with the First World War?) and settled down to the serious business of testing two lots of cooked sausages from two different caterers. This took another hour, what with savoury cakes and more drinks and a vote on the sausages. The meeting closed at almost 11pm. I couldn't wait to leave but I knew I would have to go round the room to shake hands or kiss everyone before I could gain exit. So I waited until everyone was leaving and in the general melee just kissed a few cheeks and shook a few hands within reach (but not forgetting the mayor - I am a creep) before escaping to my car. Why was this a problem for me? Why couldn't I just leave a bit earlier and go round the room saying goodbye as the French do?

These good people are slightly puzzled by us. They have been imbued with these rules of nicety since birth. Babies are quickly initiated into the routine habit of greeting any adult or older child by giving them a kiss on the cheek. The children never demur, no matter how ancient or gruesome the person is. I have vague memories of squirming when elderly, moustachioed aunts bent over me as a little child. 'Give your Auntie Mabel a kiss then.' French children, on the contrary, accept these duties without argument because everybody else does.

As schoolchildren at primary school, they walk along in a *crocodile*, two by two, holding hands in pairs (even girls and boys together) under the watchful eyes of their teachers. They kiss their parents goodnight every night whatever their age. My students are astonished that our teenage and adult children no longer do this. We were discussing this difference between English and French family manners, when I remembered something my mother said to me before my brother's wedding. She said she was looking forward to the occasion because she would get a kiss from her son. This is only remarkable because I knew he hadn't kissed his mum since he was six or seven years old. I didn't tell the group for fear of their pity for English families.

Despite living here for years now and knowing theoretically how to do it, we still cannot help our English unease in some social situations. The whole village had a day out a few weeks ago. We all went in our cars to the coast and met up for a visit to a nature centre and a restaurant meal. It was a jolly occasion and everyone got on very well. The last activity was a visit to a car museum at a chateau. Eric and I finished the tour and came out of the château wondering how to proceed. We wandered down to the little tourist shop and found ourselves back at the car park. What to do now? Wait for everyone else? But the day's outing was over. Couldn't we just leave quietly? We had conversed with everybody all day and felt that there was no need for any more song and dance.

At the next committee meeting, I was taken aside and sympathetically asked if everything had been all right for us on the day out to the seaside. 'We waited for you. We wondered where you were. We wanted to say goodbye.' I floundered and could find no adequate excuse for our seemingly unsociable behaviour.

In France, when you are sitting at a café table, you can't help noticing this hand-shaking and kissing which is part and parcel of saying hello. Most surprising of all to us English is to watch adolescents arrive and greet each other in this way without any embarrassment, or romantic or sexual nuance involved. The girl and boy could be just school pals or cousins or even brother and sister. It is a matter of social manners and the French do it with ease.

All this practice has got to make the French more confident when they come to date the opposite sex. I certainly know the agonies of shyness my son went through at this stage and realise that a French upbringing would have eased his passage into adulthood.

All this seems rather one-sided, I know. Still, it counts for a lot, and represents some of the reasons why English people come to live in France by choice. But just in case you are beginning to think the French are perfect, let me tell you that their toilets are not all that they should be.

Surely a café serving a hundred people at a time should offer more than one loo? One café in our local town of Lisieux boasts wonderful service and impeccable manners from the host and his staff, but the toilets, often far from sweet-smelling, are positioned right next to the bar, and there is a urinal in an ante-room that you have to pass to get to the one and only toilet cabinet. If there are health and safety rules, they are certainly ignored. I personally have difficulty saying *bonjour* whilst passing a gentleman's back to get to the ladies' toilet.

Moreover, have you ever seen a dog in a restaurant? Well they bring them into restaurants here, sometimes just to sit under the table, sometimes in a basket on a chair, and some friends of ours even witnessed a lady ordering food for the dog from the menu. Maybe this is simply a stage more civilised than our own society, treating animals as people, but when the French disobey their own rules of behaviour, it is worth remarking on. French people routinely ignore the 'No Dogs' sign on beaches and nobody I know has ever seen a French dog-owner do any poop-scooping.

Even worse I'm afraid, is that it is a commonplace occurrence to see a man 'admiring nature' by the side of his car. Now, women do not admire nature in the same blatant way, and I'm sure, if in need, they walk some way into the wood for cover. But not the men. The most embarrassing moment so far for me was cycling up a lane and seeing a chap facing me, in a field by a farm on the right. I nodded and said *bonjour* (I am learning). The chap nodded and replied '*Bonjour*' politely, as required by the situation. It was only as I was passing him that I saw the arc of liquid flowing from him into the grass. My steering went all wobbly.

As far as the French attitude to dog-owning is concerned, I'm convinced we Brits behave better, whereas on the subject of men's relief of nature, I'm not sure if we Brits are more civilised or simply more prudish. I am in no doubt, however, that the French interact with their fellowmen, and bring their children up in a much more polite and cohesive manner than we do. They could teach us a lot. But will we ever learn.

Holier Than Thou?
October / November 2007

You might think chrysanthemums are perfectly nice flowers to give for a birthday or to your hostess for the evening – but not here in France. Here, chrysanthemums are too closely linked with the dead. They are bought in their millions every year on the weekend nearest the 1st November (*Toussaint*) All Saints' Day. On that weekend, cemeteries and churchyards teem with families taking chrysanthemums to the graves of their dear departed.

As you look around graveyards you immediately see that the French more readily show their emotions than the British. You see photographs inset in the tombstone or propped up in frames with flowers and mementoes to the dead person. The mementoes can be personalised souvenirs like a pipe, a watch or an instrument – not real ones, but bought representations. This seems a little too maudlin if not a touch macabre to us. I personally have a tiny jolt when I pass a roadside *calvaire* or religious tableau. The figure of Christ is always daubed with blood - the more the better. There is a cadaver like this round the corner from us. My grandchildren are quite mesmerised, but I'm not sure it's for the right reasons.

We live near Lisieux, so our local *calvaires,* used in the past for prayers by workers out in the fields when the church bells rang, feature Sainte Thérèse who was canonised by Pope Pius X1 in 1925 and who spent her short, prayerful life in Lisieux. Raising her to the stature of a saint meant a lot to France after the First World War and by the nineteen thirties she had an international following and money flowed into Lisieux to build a basilica in her honour. I even remember a popular song dedicated to her in the nineteen fifties called Saint Theresa of the Roses sung by Malcolm Vaughan. Today, Lisieux is a centre of pilgrimage for Catholics all over the world and indeed the basilica is an impressive architectural feat well worth a visit.

Historically, France was so overwhelmingly catholic that the Protestants or *Huguenots* had to flee the country in past centuries, a lot of them fetching up in England. Nowadays, although there are minority religions, when a French person says he goes to church he means the Catholic Church. There is also an assumption, in the countryside at least, that when foreigners (like us) go to church, it must be a Catholic one.

This assumption causes me a little embarrassment from time to time. This is because the picturesque view from our house is so enhanced by the village church at its centre point. The church is illuminated at nightfall until midnight and I'm sure we benefit more than anyone else from this. So when I was asked to join the church preservation society I couldn't refuse. The society is struggling and only just manages to preserve the church. There is a visiting priest three times a year and the evening lights, and that is all. It seems we never have the money or the remotest possibility of restoring the age-old stones. As a member of the church preservation society, I'm expected to be there when the priest arrives to celebrate Mass. Since I am not religious I feel a hypocrite. Everyone else goes up to take communion but that is a step too far for me, so as everyone in the pew waits for me to step forward, I shake my head, mumble and make myself misunderstood once again. It isn't that the French are religious, in fact not many people under sixty are (a recent poll showed that only 5% of the population regularly practises a religion) but most people, especially in the countryside, stick to the rituals of Catholic tradition.

About three years ago, the French newspapers were full of stories about schools refusing to allow Muslim girls to wear the veil. This is just the counterpart to what happens in the UK too, but the rationale for the interdiction was quite the opposite. In the UK, the reasons given are that it is not part of the uniform, or it's against Health and Safety. In France, there are no uniforms in public and most private schools. The girls in question were simply told that no outward signs of religion were allowed in school. This is because church and state are completely separate here and have been so since 1905. There are no bishops sitting in parliament and the president is not the religious leader nor does he choose the next religious leader. Schools are neutral spaces where pupils can learn away from the pressures of party politics or religion. There was no crisis of conscience or court case over the schoolgirls, just a resolve to apply the law. The law prevailed because it was consistent and clear. Religion has no place in the school curriculum and there are no religious assemblies. Instead, in secondary schools, students study philosophy – not as a choice but as part of the core curriculum.

Wednesday was not a school day in France until President Sarkozy changed the rules and this was the day when traditionally, children went to church to receive catechism lessons from the priest. The number has been decreasing since the nineteen sixties so the majority of young people in France now know little about religion at all. We had a nineteen-year-old student staying with us in the eighties who, when doing a translation had to ask us what an 'altar' was. When I gave her the French word, she still had no idea what it was.

It seems to me a wise approach to leave young people to make up their own mind about something as personal as religion, and yet what a shame that a whole chunk of their history and heritage are no longer passed down through the generations.

A calvaire at the roadside near Saint Aubin sur Algot

The Proof Of The Pudding
December 2007 / January 2008

I read last month that Gordon Ramsay is going to open a restaurant in Paris in the New Year. Nothing extraordinary about that, but hey – its unique selling point will be that it will serve *British* food. I wonder if he will succeed where others have not dared. I saw the teams from The Apprentice go over with their English cheese and sausages and try to sell them on a French market. And I saw how bemused their French customers looked at the very idea.

I have asked French people why they don't buy English cheeses and why they seem impervious to our attempts to introduce our produce, only to have them give a Gallic shrug and tell me they have so much good and varied food in France they don't need to look abroad for other culinary experiences. In this respect, the French are much more patriotic than we are. All they need to do, if they want to try something different is to visit another town to try something different – each town or area has its own *spécialité*.

Even when an occasional dish does pass muster, like *le crumble* which has become popular in France over the last ten years (served as a cold dessert), they are totally unaware that it's a British recipe. They think it must be a new French invention.

'I've had a belly-full of the French coming over here and telling us what s*** our food is,' said Gordon in an interview with The Sunday Times, 'they just have posher names.' I suppose he meant that we have cheese on toast, they have *croque-monsieur*; we have cottage pie, they have *hachis Parmentier*.

It is certainly true that British cooking has a poor reputation in France. If British food is mentioned in conversation, you can see the flicker of amusement behind the politeness. 'Is it true you eat jam with meat?' they ask.
'Well', I reply, 'we do serve apple sauce with pork and cranberry sauce with turkey at Christmas, but don't you have a famous dish called *canard à l'orange*?'
'That's different. It's a traditional recipe. Anyway, you English, you boil all your meat and vegetables until they taste of nothing.'

Where has this myth come from I wonder? I try to explain that we certainly don't boil all our meat, but we do cook it more thoroughly than they do, in fact, we think they don't cook it enough.

For many years I was involved in accompanying teenagers to and from France on twinning exchanges. The French teenagers thought the banana or mashed egg sandwiches that their hostesses gave them were like vomit and they concluded after their week that we English ate only pizza or hamburgers with lots of chips. The only thing they did enjoy was the full English breakfast.

On the other hand, our English youngsters thought it was disgusting to have to face meat that was red in the middle or even leaking bloody juices, fish with their heads on, and to have to drink only water with meals instead of coke or juice. They didn't know what to do when faced with a packed lunch of a hard-boiled egg (still in its shell) and half a baguette. They did like sitting down with all their French family round the table though. It's an uphill struggle trying to rescue our reputation for bad food, so can Gordon do it?

According to Christian Constant, a top French chef who owns four restaurants in Paris, Gordon is wrong. It's not just that the French give fancy names to ordinary dishes, it's that they raise ordinary dishes to new heights by the skill of their cooking. 'We are connoisseurs. We know what we are talking about'.

This argument began to sink in when I came to Normandy and was presented in a restaurant with the local speciality – *tripes à la mode de Caen*. Now, I remember eating tripe when I was a kid in Burnley. It was white and very chewy and had practically no taste. I also got the impression that it was food from the old days when people couldn't afford proper meat. I couldn't have been more surprised when the dish put in front of me was nothing like my memory or tripe. This was cooked in a delicious sauce and given lots of unctuous taste. It had been raised to the level of a special dish. If the French chef is right, then what is important in France is what you do to the food you eat, and French people certainly do know.

I have tested this, not exactly scientifically, but whenever I ask the question, 'What is your favourite food?' a typical English person might say, 'fish and chips', 'a good steak', or 'roast beef and Yorkshire pudding'. My French guinea-pig however will give me the recipe step by step of say, scallops with white wine sauce and parsley. Then, they will fall to arguing with each other over the best way to cook them. They all will have an opinion. They have all cooked and eaten a much wider range of foodstuffs than the average

Brit. The skills of preparation and sauce-making, especially for savoury dishes (which usually means meat or fish in some form as vegan / vegetarians are rare in France) is a national interest and entrenched in their culture.

And this knowledge and love of cooking has nothing to do with being well off or not. We have been invited to eat in sumptuous villas, tiny council flats in the Paris suburbs and simple homes, like a wooden cabin built by the railway sidings. They may have had different furnishings but every home had the table in pride of place and every housewife (or husband for that matter), produced food cooked with the 'correct' accompaniment and washed down with the finest wines. Every home had a wine-cellar too.

It is no use telling me that we English used to have sophisticated dishes before the last world war and that it's because of the rationing that we lost all our skills and confidence. Didn't France have rationing too? In fact, according to my French teacher in the sixties, things were so bad in Paris during the war that people were reduced to eating the rats. However, I'm sure the accompanying sauce was just right.

British cooking, is not the same thing as British food. The raw materials, the ingredients, shouldn't be confused with our lack of tradition for sophisticated preparation. As Gordon Ramsay says, 'We should stand strong and shout from the rooftops about our phenomenal venison from Balmoral and our wonderful Aberdeen Angus steaks.' I would add to that our marvellous Welsh lamb and indeed all our home-grown produce.

There is a good reason why our meat and vegetables and fruit are in fact, superb. The climate in the UK is temperate and the land rich and well-watered, There is no arid season at all and no snow of any duration to prevent cultivation. There has always been a plentiful supply of seasonal foods. Consequently there has never been much reason to improve on those fine ingredients. A fine steak needs little embellishment. Your standard meat and two veg cooked simply with nothing added but a little salt and pepper and a curl of butter is what we all know from our grandparents as 'good, plain cooking'.

It is understandable that in hotter countries, before the age of refrigeration, people developed ways to disguise the taste of the meat as it began to go off. India, Mexico and Africa are all places where the cuisine includes fantastic use of spices. These dishes are fabulously tasty but it's easy to work out why the need for them arose. Of course France is not such an extreme example, but large parts of the country are hot and arid in summer and they must have experimented with ways to make the food more palatable rather than waste it.

So my argument is that British food is as good as French food any day. There is a town in Normandy called Mortagne-au-Perche whose *spécialité* is *boudin noir*. This particular town has taken the celebration of its speciality to such heights that they have an international competition. So what is this speciality, *Boudin noir?* Well, it's nothing but good old black pudding. *Boudin* (the derivation of the English word 'pudding') started in France as a savoury hot dish, came over to England and became a hot dessert (and is now on its way back over to France in the form of *le crumble*).

In Mortagne-au-Perche at the food festival, we wandered, bemused, around the marquees, seeing all the judges in white coats looking at, and tasting, rows and rows of these savoury puddings, both black and white, laid out on trestle-tables with awards attached to the lucky few samples. Imagine our incredulity when we saw that the international award for best black pudding went to a town in the north-west of England called Bury.

If it's a question of pleasing the customer in a restaurant with how you cook and serve the food, then I'm not sure how Gordon will fare. However, if it's a question of the quality of the foodstuff itself, then if Bury can steal the gold medal from the French, then go for it, Gordon. What are you waiting for?

Foire au boudin in Mortagne-au-Perche

Black puddings in Bury, Lancashire

Home Sweet Home
February / March 2008

As more and more Brits buy properties in France, either for holidays or as a permanent move, maybe some of our readers regularly dream of a house in France. After going through the process twice, plus interpreting for plenty of others, I'd like to offer my bit of advice. See what you think...

We chose Normandy both times because it's hot enough for us. Also, we can drive to England within hours if need be. In the middle of the Pays d'Auge we are only 1½ hours by train from Paris and within ½ hour of the sea. There are historic chateaux, unspoilt beaches, upmarket resorts like Deauville and Cabourg and excellent shops in Caen and Rouen.

You can, believe it or not, tire of the simple life and I have seen too many English couples buying a property in the middle of nowhere and then going to pieces for lack of human contact. Having different types of venue to visit nearby adds variety to your life and to your friends' holiday visits too. If you live in the countryside, a day out is more likely to be to a sizeable town – after all, you have the countryside on your doorstep all the time. In Normandy, the Orne department is much more isolated than the Calvados (shown on the map below), and that is reflected in the house prices. After all, not many French people want to be isolated either.

In the Calvados, there are two main types of traditional architecture. Within stone-carting distance of Caen, the traditional building material is the beautiful creamy-white stone which bears its name. So prized was this stone that not only were the major religious and defensive constructions in Caen, Falaise and Domfront built of it, but William the Conqueror had it taken over to England. The White Tower in London is so called because it's built of Caen stone. For domestic buildings, these stones are generously cemented with creamy mastic – they call it 'buttering' and the effect is a clean, warm and solid homely structure.

Away from Caen, in the Pays d'Auge, between the rivers Dives and Touques, half-timbered houses abound. These are houses *en colombage*. Wood has always been plentiful in this area and the Vikings, who settled here in the early Middle-Ages, simply transferred their boat-building skills to houses. Some of these houses have thatched roofs too. You can see the connection when you visit the wooden church of St Catherine's in Honfleur and look at the twin ceilings which look exactly like the bottom of two upturned boats.

It's important to consider how far you are prepared to live from the nearest amenities. I haven't taken my own advice on this point. On both occasions when buying, I muttered in vain about being able to walk into a village with at least a *boulangerie*. But to no avail. Each time the house's attractions overcame my objections. The result is that it's harder to feel part of a community, particularly when you haven't children at home. Also, one car may not prove to be enough if one of the couple starts to work away from the house. So, location really is everything, especially for a new life in France.

My French students always ask, when on the subject of houses, why English people rarely seem to buy property in the towns. My theory is that most of us have to go back at least six generations before we discover an ancestor who lived on the land. A large proportion of the population moved into the towns during the industrial revolution. Countryside living is a romantic dream for us. The French, in contrast, remain largely an agricultural nation right up to the present. Most of my students, although in modern jobs in town, have parents or grandparents still living in the country. So, up to very recently, the reality of the countryside was enough to propel young French people into the towns. It isn't that they don't like or respect the countryside, it's just that they understand its limitations. And anyway, a lot of French families own a property in the countryside collectively, inherited from a previous generation, where they meet up for a holiday in August. That is probably enough countryside for them.

Moving to France permanently is a different game altogether from buying a holiday home. If it is to be your only home, your needs are very different. It's a fact that you can tell you are in a holiday home immediately you are shown inside. First, there's the smell. With the best will in the world, if nobody is there most of the time and there is no heating, it will smell musty. There is usually a lack of practical living-space: such as where the laundry is done, DIY tools are kept or food is stored. When you are spending your two weeks' holiday barbecuing in the garden, what does it matter if the kitchen cupboards are primitive or non-existent? A lovely, open, wood fire is certainly attractive but what about real heating for the winter? A holiday home is unlikely to offer the comforts you have been used to like good insulation against heat and cold, double-glazing and reliable plumbing.

Those original floor-tiles may have the desirable patina of old-age, but they will be very uneven, difficult to keep clean and will wear out rugs that you need to put down to be warm and cosy in winter. Old, planked internal doors look the business but will clatter every time you close them and will let a thousand draughts through.

A lot of old country cottages were not intended for living in upstairs. Upstairs was simply a hay loft, or storage. The reverse is true in mountain villages in the Alps - the ground floor was for the animals and the first floor for the humans. The result is that many a renovated house will have bedrooms *d'affilée* - that is, you have to walk through one bedroom to get to the next as there is no corridor. This is all right for families with small children but very awkward otherwise. The bathroom has often been installed downstairs because it was easier to plumb in on the ground floor – an inconvenient convenience.

In short, I suspect that what a lot of us really, really want is olde-worlde charm with modern standards of building and comfort. You just need to acknowledge what conditions you are prepared to live in. Don't be blinkered when looking in those estate agents' windows. You are going to get a bargain anyway since the properties you look at will be far cheaper than similar ones in the UK.

Why not look at a couple of modern ones too – if only to discount them. At least you will have seen inside and be in a position to compare the living arrangements with those of old houses. Sometimes, what you lose in character you gain in amenities and living space. For example, a house built since the fifties may well have a basement which is a large as the whole of the ground floor. It can offer garaging, a laundry room, an extra shower-room, a workshop or a playroom or even a teenager's bedroom.

You might consider, instead of old-world charm renovated to a high standard, a new house built in a traditional style. A house of this type cost us the equivalent of £170,000 in 2002 and was built in the traditional manner of half-timbered houses in the Pays d'Auge with 32 tons of oak, has plenty of bedrooms, three bathrooms, double-glazing, central heating, a traditional fireplace, insulation in roof walls and between the floors to eliminate noise and creaking, and even a central vacuuming system. It was built specifically to capture a ravishing view. That's the theory. So we decided to go down this route ourselves and buy a modern house.

There can be another drawback though. It's not unusual to find the 'gardens' in the countryside can be 3 acres and more. That's another mistake we English make – we're suckers for land. So one final decision for you to make – how much land are you willing to manage? Land in the French countryside is, on the whole, cheap. I know it hits the spot when you stand at the top of a stretch of land and think, 'All this is mine!' After all, an Englishman's home is his castle. This is especially true if, like us, you have lived in towns and had small gardens, and what's more, you get a fabulous view from your house.

The fact is you spend much more of your time doing ground maintenance than actual gardening. By that I mean, by the time you have cut the acres of grass by tractor, and have cut the areas by push-mover that can't be cut by the tractor, and strimmed the rest of the grass that you can't do otherwise, you move onto the hedge-trimmer to prune the forty or so bushes, coppicing the tree-tall hedges. You never seem to get round to the finer details of dead-heading the flowers or transferring plants to a better location.

It just goes to show, that when it comes to France, your heart really does rule your head.

A traditional Normandy house en colombage

Our house – a modern colombage

Education, Education, Education
April / May 2008

Schools have been bombarded in the UK with changes over the last twenty years: national curriculum, 'maths hours', 'literature hours', exams changing all the time and Tony Blair announcing that he wanted 50% of all 18 year-olds to go to university. So what is schooling like in France?

Well, the French have had a national curriculum since the turn of the last century, and it is so precise and detailed, it is said that a visitor can go into any classroom, anywhere in France and know what the teacher will be doing with the class at that moment in time.

Compulsory schooling doesn't start until six, but the provision of state nurseries, attached to primary schools is so generous, that almost all children start school at around three years old. However, your child won't be taught any letters or numbers until the prescribed age of six, no matter how forward and eager your child is to learn. In the first year of school proper, at age six, your child must apply himself to joined-up writing straight away. The curriculum must be followed to the letter.

Is this a good thing? Well, it is easier for parents to know what their child will be learning and as well as being obliged to buy all the necessary books on the curriculum, they can buy also buy extra books, labelled with the subject and level (*CM2* for example, for ten year-olds) of work they are expected to do. It's good for teachers too, to have everything laid down and nothing left to chance. The teacher doesn't have to prepare different work for children who learn at different speeds – they just all do the same; there are no table groupings doing less or more challenging work.

On the other hand, woe betide the child who doesn't get the grade at the end of the year; they'll be kept down a year. This is called *redoublement*. I'm not sure what it would have done to my confidence to be in a class with pupils one or even two years younger than me.

For this reason, parents are anxious that their child should keep up with the rest of the class. This means that they supervise their children's homework every evening, and homework is given every day from the age of 6. I don't mean just conscientious, middle-class parents either; I mean all parents, with very, very few exceptions. Homework is considered the responsibility of parents. If they work long hours, or are unsure themselves about their children's homework, they often pay students to do the job for them.

Even during the holidays, parents buy the very popular magazine *Cahier des Vacances* to go over what was learned in the last year, so the child doesn't forget last year's lessons and is ready for the next. That's what you get for having eight weeks holiday in summer.

Contrast this with Britain, where, in my experience, as a pupil, parent and a teacher, homework is considered the responsibility of the school. That is, I as a parent might ask 'Have you done your homework?' now and again, but ultimately, if my child hasn't done the homework, I know it's the teacher's job to sanction my child.

As a child at school in France, the great thing is you don't have to wear a uniform. In England, the uniform has infiltrated even primary schools. On the other hand, there is quite a strict notion of what is appropriate dress in French schools – no skirts up to the bottom or revealing tops, or thongs appearing over the back of the jeans.

An interesting situation has arisen over the last two decades about the subject of what you can and can't wear at school. In the UK there are cases of Muslim girls wanting to wear the hijab headscarf but the school protesting that it isn't part of the school uniform. There have been various court decisions – some saying yes they could, and some saying no they couldn't. I don't know whether a consensus has been reached on the matter.

In France, the situation is quite clear. No outward religious symbols must been worn in state schools. Why? Because the Catholic Church (most French people, if they practise a religion, tend to be Catholic) and state have been separated since before the beginning of the twentieth century. Public (as in, not private) schools are an institution of the state and religion must not be taught in any way. Religion is a private matter and school is for the development of the individual as citizen. Instead of religion, pupils study philosophy in the upper secondary school as an obligatory subject. So the wearing of religious symbols is not accepted and this is enshrined in the law. There was no hesitation about banning the hijab from schools and it no longer appears to be a problem.

The French school day is long, and can be from 8.00.am to 5.30pm at secondary school. You see children waiting for school buses as early as 7am. The public is also allowed to use the school buses and I think that contributes to better behaviour on them – something for the authorities to think about in the UK. Teachers have it easier because they are contracted to teach 21, 18 or 15 contact hours a week according to how well-qualified they are. If they have a free hour or two during the day, they can go shopping, go to the gym or with a bit of luck, meet a lover.

So these outward signs might lead you to think French schoolchildren are more individualistic, maybe more rebellious – no religion taught to them, no uniform to wear. The amazing thing is they are not. They are on the whole very polite, with one another and with adults. At primary school level, they must hold hands in pairs (even boys) and walk in a *crocodile* when out and about with a teacher. I saw a group of secondary school pupils with their teachers waiting in a busy Paris railway station. They were all sitting cross-legged on the floor in a group. I suspect their English counterparts would be wandering around out of the sight of the teachers.

So what is it that ensures that all French students come out of the other end of the educational system as obedient, civilised people who all have lunch at 12, know their *cuisine*, and kiss their parents every day?

If I knew the whole explanation I'd be rich as lots of countries would like their population to be like this (I exclude the political protests, but they only do this because their unions *tell* them to) I believe a lot of it has to do with the inflexibility of the curriculum and the system. It all starts in primary school.

Children do not take lunchboxes to school. They eat in the canteen, where they are served a balanced four-course meal every day. This continues at secondary school. Consequently there are very few vegetarians, food allergies or overweight children – a result of the 'one-size fits all' education.

But there is a down side. You are in danger of having your uniqueness flattened out by learning everything the same way and at the same time, having to learn the 'correct' literary interpretations, as given in the study books, and how important it is to colour within the lines (tell that to Cezanne!) A French child has to have the most robust, unassailable confidence. They must remember that it is not a teacher's or boss's role to encourage their creativity or initiative. All through school and university you are marked out of 20. That is, the teacher starts at 20 and knocks off a mark for every mistake as he sees it. So French youngsters are quite used to getting 8/20 and are ecstatic with 12/20 as this will be the top mark in the class. For dictations, minus marks are common. I would be a snivelling psychiatric case if I'd had to undergo this treatment for 15 years - but not the average French person. Why, they even continue to do dictations just for fun, as a community game when they are adults. Think this will take on in the bingo halls?

Did I say 15 years? Sorry, I mean 20 years schooling all together, since no decent job can be had unless you've done four or more years at university level. Kids don't leave home here until they're at least 25 (that's for the first time). Not like those who in England leave at 18 to go to university, shack up with a girlfriend, break up and lose the job at 25 then come back home – by then, the French youth hasn't even left. There's no worry over getting into university, you'll be glad to hear. No need for Tony Blair's 50% target, at least 70% go to university in France. In France, students have the right to go to a university, without any interview, as long as they have their *baccalauréat* (A levels). What is more, they go to the nearest university so that they can live at home if possible or at least come home at weekends. Parents again accept the responsibility of lodging their children until all those studies are complete. What am I saying? Parents are obliged by law to contribute to the maintenance of their offspring until the age of 26 if the child is in full-time education. There have been numerous law cases of children taking their parents to court for maintenance.

So if your twenty-one year olds are complaining about student loans, don't show them this article, it might give them ideas.

10 Two Parties
June / July 2008

'It's now or never. It might never happen again. It must be fifteen years or more since all the family were gathered together. You've got to do it, mum.'

This is how my daughter enthused, urged and emotionally blackmailed me into deciding on a party. She did have a point – well several really. All five of our children were dispersed over the globe; a daughter in Australia, another daughter near Geneva, a son in South Africa and a son and daughter in Chorley and Skipton.

Eric was going to be seventy and I sixty in April this year - not something to shout from the rooftops I know and we had never gone in for big 'dos' but what Amy said struck a chord. Before I knew it, I had said yes and she had designed the invitations and drawn up a guest list.

I never thought of any other venue than our garden. A hotel room or the village hall (which is the usual place for family parties in France) would be too impersonal and anyway, I had already started to daydream about a marquee and all our friends at their elegant best sipping champagne on the lawn. Nearer to April, practicalities loomed large: how to seat 90 people? The French are not happy to balance a pork pie and a Bakewell tart on a paper plate and call it a meal.

So, at the next committee meeting for our association *pour mieux se connaitre* (to get to know each other better) I hesitatingly mentioned our idea. *'Pas de problème!'* Two days before the party two men, employed by the village, arrived with the old wooden trestle tables and benches which must have served the village during two world wars judging from the rough wood and drawing pins punctuating their surface. As we helped to unload we recognised one of the chaps was the man who tends all the public flower beds and lives with his mother in a tumbledown cottage buried in flowers and where the door is always open. Frederic has learning difficulties. He does his job seriously and conscientiously and the village looks after him and respects him, as it should.

The day before the party, friends were already arriving from England. The house was full plus an overflow campervan on the drive. Then the wind got up and before long the roof of the marquee was flapping about dangerously. Initiative was called for and plastic dishes were used to cover the holes and insert the roof poles.

We couldn't afford full catering and I couldn't prepare a full meal for all those people so a compromise was called for. We found a lovely couple on the market cooking couscous and paella in enormous dishes. They agreed to come and cook on the spot for a very reasonable sum. A local friend recommended a jazz band which I was able to contact through a web-site well-used by the expats in Normandy (normandy.angloinfo.com). One scroll down the forum page on this site aptly describes the concerns of Brits over here: 'Pot-bellied Vietnamese pigs for sale; advice on inheritance laws needed; anyone interested in starting a Morris-dancing group in the Manche?'

After weeks of rain, frost and wind, the day dawned fair and calm. Cars snaked up the drive, locals arrived on foot pressing flowers and presents and cards on us. Our two biggest grandchildren did a great job in charge of car-parking in the field and chocolate eggs were hidden around the garden for the younger children to hunt for when things began to flag.

Our local French friends were rather perplexed by the timing of the party – afternoon? But what meal could that be? Meal times are set in stone in France and this event would be neither at lunchtime nor dinner. We had decided on the afternoon because, in April, the afternoon afforded the best chance of reasonable warmth.

As soon as the *kir royal* (champagne with blackcurrant liqueur) kicked in, the bonhomie blossomed. French and English mingled with laughter and friends and family from all over England renewed their ties and were amazed at how little everybody had changed.

There is a class system in France as in England. People often don't realise that when they come to live over here. They think they are simply all French. I had invited some local village friends and also some very bourgeois French friends too. These latter are mostly well-off Parisians who have a country house around here. They don't usually go to the local 'dos'. However, there were no restraints at all, everyone chatted to everyone with only their expensive hairdos and Barbour jackets to give some of them away.

The jazz band arrived after missing their way a bit and soon charmed us all with their music. The jazz fans amongst the guests showed us how to trip the light fantastic. Bob Tinker was the trumpet player and leader of the band. Guess where he hails from? Preston, Lancashire! I wondered what had brought him to live in Normandy but there was little time to gossip. There were two French instrumentalists, one American and one Lancastrian, so it was a triumph of *entente cordiale*.

After the *crudités* and pâté starters, there were the go-and-get-your-own couscous or paella from the wagon, and the cheeses (Camembert and Livarot local cheeses and of course Lancashire brought over especially). The desserts were all made by my friends, so along with Tiramisu and mouth-watering English dishes like cheesecakes (French reaction – 'Cheese? Cake? In the same word? How can this be?'), there were also two giant pots of *teurgoule*, the local speciality. Now I know that Müller have made a fortune selling cold rice pudding, but this takes the biscuit. There is a thick crocodile brown skin and it has to be knocked senseless onto your plate. So I was amazed to see how the English took to it. I saw Carole scraping the bowl out after the party. Carole by the way, is Eric's daughter who flew on her own all the way from near Brisbane, leaving her two girls and her husband, just to be with us. She was fantastic and everything would not have come together had she not taken me in hand and made crucial decisions, dressed the tables and spent all morning with me preparing *crudités* (and that's not what I called them when I had finished!).

The sun started to go down. Son Robin and daughter Amy said a few words in English and French respectively, the couscous couple left all the leftovers in my big pans, the Jazz Band played 'Every Time I Say Goodbye' and guests trickled back down the drive. Son Mike turned up the stereo and first up dancing on the tables was Eric's cousin, Barbara, respectable teacher of the parish of Fence near Nelson. I couldn't believe it. Carole was doing cartwheels on the lawn and I couldn't resist the inexplicable magnetism of The Maverick's 'I Want to Dance the Night Away'. I didn't quite dance the night away.

The following Saturday the French locals showed us how to really party. It was the regular spring fete in the village hall. I had to get involved because they had just lent us all the tables and benches for our 'do'. So, after I had done my four hours putting up the tables and decorating the room in the afternoon with the other ladies, we arrived at eight pm. Children as old as ten came up to us to be kissed. Everybody who arrived shook hands or kissed everybody else. The evening unfolded unhurriedly with *apéritifs*, *choucroute*, cheeses and fruit salad. Incidentally, in the afternoon, the ladies taught me how to prepare lettuce properly. They cut out the spine of each leaf until well into the middle, having pulled off the top of the outer leaves as they are thought too tough. Then they cut down the spine to make two parts of each small leaf. Yes, well...

The DJ played an eclectic range of music from the usual French accordion fifties stuff, to the incongruous, 'Here We Go, Here We Go, Here We Go' raucously sung along to by the crowd on the dance floor. I say crowd because the DJ had no trouble getting people up to dance. That's what they were there for- that and eating and being expertly sociable around the room. Surprisingly little wine was drunk – we were the first group to buy a bottle. These days the French are much more health conscious than they used to be. In fact, the English have overtaken them as far as wine consumption goes.

The average age was about mine and yet, totally unlike Peter Kay's elderly relatives who want to get home at 8pm to close the curtains and settle in, this lot were unknockdownable. It was ten minutes to one in the morning. We had just served dessert ('Don't rush it, they are enjoying themselves', said our kitchen leader) and coffee was about an hour and a half away. Still they were dancing. We were shattered. I was really shattered as I had been serving and collecting dishes all night. On the way round serving, one or two foxy old chaps had demanded a kiss for forgetting something, or had leapt up and insisted on dancing. A moustachioed old chap had been going around giving a flower (pinched from the table decorations) as blackmail to any lady he fancied dancing with. Well you could have knocked me down with a feather when he came up to us and asked, not me, but Eric, to dance! I kid you not. When Eric flustered and refused he asked Mike, my son. Mike went even redder and I had to get up to save their faces. I haven't personally witnessed that before so I cannot report for sure dear reader, that this is part of the old French tradition, or whether, as Eric said afterwards, he is just an eccentric.

Eric and me with the jazz band

The French party

Little Things Mean A Lot
August / September 2008

Why do you not see flowers in the windows of French houses, in spite of the French buying cut flowers more often than we do? And why are there often no curtains? For the answers to these and other little differences between French and English homes and lifestyles, read on.

In France, the first thing you notice as you walk up to your house is the size of the garden. There is more land per head of population in France, therefore land is cheap and you get more around each house. An acre is nothing over here. If you want to be lord of all you survey, remember it will severely change your lifestyle if you come from a suburban garden setting. There are hedges to cut and trees to coppice. If those trees overhang the telephone lines, you will be told in writing to see to them or pay the bill when they do it. Grass grows. You can't get away from that, so you will have to pay someone to do it if you are not there and if you are there you will spend many hours a week cutting it. Yes, you can come to an arrangement with the local farmer who might cut it once a year and take the hay, but should you wish to rescind the arrangement in later years, you may have established a right over your land you never intended to. You can keep sheep / goats / donkeys to eat the grass but do you know how much vets charge and how much responsibility animals are?

The next things you notice are the shutters on the outside of the windows. They come in various styles: wind-down or electric roller types, wooden concertina-types doors or single, hinged panels. They are used to keep out the cold, the heat, prying eyes of neighbours and burglars and are quite effective at all that. In summer, you can leave the windows open and the shutters closed. This allows the air to circulate and keeps out most insects. French people close the shutters around the house every night and this can mean a half an hour's work. You have to apply some wood treatment every three years or so because the sun dries out the wood, so more work there.

Because you have shutters, there is no need for curtains. Our house had never had curtains before we came and we have only put up a few to make us feel at home. Needless to say, we never close them. So if you don't have curtains you avoid a lot of expense and save on dry-cleaning too. It seems there is more work but less money to spend on French houses. Here's another example, windows open inwards which means you can reach the outside as well as the inside for cleaning. So there are no professional window-cleaners for the domestic market, which saves you a bill but means you have more window-cleaning to do and nobody else to blame for the state of them.

What is more, there are rarely window sills on the inside, so no room for ornaments and bric-a-brac. Great! Much less dusting all round. And now I know why loads of English people love the car-boot sales over here – they are surely not buying, they are selling, getting rid of all the stuff accrued over the years on their window sills in England A lot of French people open their bedroom windows for a while every morning and duvets are thrown out over the sill to be aired. This is an acquired skill and you need to be totally above caring what the neighbours think of your taste in duvet-covers.

Inside the house, you will take off your shoes or clatter on the floors throughout on the ground floor. This is how the French like their floors. True enough, it is very hygienic being able to mop to your heart's content. We found, however that our sofas rolled around on the tiles and that there was no feeling of warmth and cosiness in winter, so we bought carpet in the UK and had a local *tapissier* in to fit it. He spent three days in the one room tacking wooden strips along the edges of the room and sewing and fitting the carpet. He did a fabulous job because he is a skilled craftsman who upholsters chairs and lines walls with tapestries but the bill was more than the cost of the carpet! I know a lot of French people don't like the idea of fitted carpets; they say they are nothing but *un nid de poussière* (a nest of dust). However, the French have taken to fitted carpets in bedrooms, but there is no underfelt and the top carpet is simply stuck to the floor leaving raw edges round the sides. Not quite the luxury you are used to in the UK.

One thing the French can teach us is how to mop those tiled floors. They have had a few centuries' practice after all. They don't use a circular mop head in a bucket with a sieve-like top; they don't use a squeegee sponge either. They use a floor-cloth (an old hand-towel will do) which is dunked in hot water and wrung out by hand, then rubbed over the floor by pushing it around with a long, stiff brush. This gives just the right purchase on the floor to get off any sticky bits and leaves the surface hardly wet at all, so that it dries in two minutes. I can't do better than that.

Of course, that tiled floor is sensible because, in the countryside, there will be an open fire. In fact I haven't really solved the problem of hot sparks occasionally shooting onto the carpet, and resort to an old rug in front of the fire. The fire will use wood and not coal. You will either have to cut down your own wood and stock it for a year before burning it, or buy it in quantities of *stères*. These are cubic measurements of approximately one metre cubed. The wood is stacked with great care along a hedge or under the overhanging gable-end which is there for that purpose.

There is good wood and bad wood and you avoid pine as there is too much resin which clogs up the chimney. Good wood is oak, apple or pear. You stock the wood in long piles about head height, turning the logs 90 degrees at each end to stabilise the whole pile. The longer your pile, the more you announce your prosperity and good-husbandry to your neighbours. So you see, size does matter.

When you want to bring enough wood into the house for the week to be ready to throw on the fire, you might well bring in into the basement. The *sous-sol,* as it is called, is nearly always a feature of late twentieth century houses. It can be as big as the whole of the ground floor and be used for just about anything: a workshop, a garage, a pantry, a games-room, an extra bedroom and bathroom and even an extra kitchen for outdoor meals. The design is quite clever as you don't need to enter the house at basement level, you can go in and out of the front and back doors straight into the garden, but that extra floor gives you so much more room at little extra cost. Having said that, not all modern French homes have a *sous-sol* - ours hadn't, so we have had to store our weekly supply of wood at the back of the 'cave' for storing the wine. I don't understand why you don't see this sort of basement in the UK, especially since there is far less available land for building.

Back inside after your daily gardening / wood-carting / shuttering jobs, you decide to have a shower. You've just dropped your dirty clothes on the floor and realise you need to spend a penny. Damn! You have to throw a towel round you (if visitors are around) and creep down the corridor to the loo. For some reason the toilet is normally separate from the bathroom. This is a good idea if there is only one bathroom as it means the toilet is always available at short notice. But the practice has continued as houses have now got two or even three bathrooms.

If the bathroom is modern-ish, you can bet there are twin washbasins so that you and your partner can scrub up together. I don't know if this has caught on in the UK but it's very popular here. It's when contemplating those twin washbasins that I'm glad the loo isn't in the bathroom after all.

You will want to put your dirty clothes in the washing machine. Well that is likely to be right at hand in the bathroom, and not in the kitchen. Of course the house may be huge and have a laundry room, but if not, it makes sense to have it in the bathroom. I mean, dirty washing has nothing to do with food, has it?

If it's normal to have the washing-machine in the bathroom, there must be an electric socket in there. That's right. French regulations allow for this. Any problem and the mains fuse box in the house will cut off completely. Individual plugs don't have an earth. Maybe this is why it's okay to have electric sockets in the bathroom. This is a boon. You can dry your hair in there, do all your epilating (not as exciting as it sounds, I'm afraid) in there. All that can be done without annoying a sleeping partner in the bedroom, unless the partner is at the other washbasin, which is the best case yet against twin washbasins.

All in all, less expense but more daily work in a French house. Maybe that's why French people are slimmer. Oops! Now I've done it. I'll have to try to justify that in the next issue – or eat my own words.

Our typical French inward-opening windows

Jack and Odile's typical French drawing room

12 Food For Thought
September / October 2008

I was on a train last month from Paris to Marseille (excellent service by the way only three hours to cover the 800 or so kilometres). Having got up very early and changed trains in Paris I was ready for something to eat. As I was uncrinkling the foil on my banana sarnies, I was embarrassed at the sound I was making, echoing round the neighbouring seats. Apart from an odd murmuring voice on a mobile, all was quiet. Why was I the only one making eating noises? Because it wasn't lunchtime of course. In fact it was about 11.30am. When I had finished and the smell of banana had abated, it was as though somebody had blown a whistle; people got up and walked along the aisle, paper bags containing ham baguettes were waved aloft and upturned water bottles bobbed up and down over the backs of seats (water that is, not juice or coke). This was because it was after 12 O'clock and everyone, in France that is, knows this is lunchtime. Not before twelve and not after 1.30pm.

Last week I promised the grandchildren we'd go to McDonalds if they were good in the supermarket first. My daughter warned me that we should go to *Macdo's* first. Why? Because it would be quiet until twelve. 'Nonsense,' I said, driving past the empty car park. At 12.20pm when we came back, the car park was packed and the queues at the five tills inside were six people deep each. They don't think like we do, the French. We'd have our lunch earlier or later to avoid all this, but they don't. Meal times, especially lunch, are sacrosanct.

At this very minute, I am writing this piece in the cafe of a *LeClerc* supermarket (it's cheap – just about £1.20 for a Danish pastry and a cup of tea). I am the only person eating anything. It is ten minutes to twelve.

I thought the train incident was funny and brought it up in conversation with French friends. 'Why should you eat when it is not a mealtime?' They asked in response, puzzled and not at all amused.

I have realised that eating only at meal-times is part of the reason why the French are winners in the health stakes. They are thinner than we are and much thinner than Americans are. How do I know this?

For the last five years I've been using an article in the English lessons I teach, about a study done on this subject in 2002, which recorded that only 7% of French people were obese, compared to 22% of Americans. I thought I'd better see if the situation is the same now for the article I'm writing for you.

Guess what? The situation is worse. We, in the UK have more than twice the number of fatties than in France. The figures don't include under 15s and only count adults with a BMI greater than 30 (which is not just overweight, it is obese).

Here are the figures:

USA: 31% of adults are obese
UK: 23% of adults are obese
FRANCE: 9% of adults are obese

Why should that be? - Especially when French food includes extremely rich recipes such as *confit de canard, foie gras* and those huge patisseries. Apparently, the French actually eat more fat than the Americans, so how come they are so much thinner?

One reason is exemplified by the train story. French people only eat at meal-times, they don't snack in between. You rarely see people eating in the street (and so there is much less litter too). We walked around a thronging market town on Saturday and during those two hours (including people-watching from a pavement café) we saw no-one eating outside. Do that experiment in a busy town on a Saturday morning in the UK. I would be interested in your findings.

This rule applies to children too. They don't eat between meals and don't eat outside. When a toddler whines a bit in the supermarket, the mother will break off the end of a baguette for them to chew on. Bread. Dry bread. Not a biscuit or crisps or chocolate. When was the last time you saw a toddler eating dry bread in England?

Oops! It is 12.05 and there is a queue of twenty at the cafe. My table will be needed shortly as people are coming in to have lunch, and lunch is serious.

When it is time to eat, the French take their food seriously. They don't eat a sandwich for lunch at their desk or make do with a cup-a–soup. In fact, lunch is the most substantial meal of the day. People go home from the office or factory if they can. If not, they go to their parents' home if it is nearby. Failing that they go to the restaurant. Yes! A restaurant, during the week, not as a special treat. They do this because they believe nutrition and a break from work is very important.

Because of this, you see women eating alone in restaurants much more than in England. They feel they have every right to be there and do not feel out of place. Eating in a restaurant is possible because it can be very cheap. At *Le Gentleman* in Lisieux, you can have two courses for €8 (about £6). The food will be made on the premises, not bought in, frozen or reheated. It won't be industrially produced either, which makes it more natural and healthy.

So there is an argument for the quality of food eaten. There is much less industrially-prepared food in France. Restaurants cook from raw ingredients, even McDonald's have had to upgrade their hamburgers for the French market. People buy very few ready-made meals – if you look round the supermarkets, you won't see anything like the choice there is in the UK. When people buy 'ready-made' it's usually from the local *patisserie / boulangerie* where the sandwiches and cakes and pâtés are made by the shop without additives and trans fats.

So, French people eat at mealtimes only – breakfast, lunch and dinner, although schoolchildren have *gouter* after school because they won't be having dinner until around eight in the evening. When they do eat, they eat a proper meal around a proper dining table. In a French home, the dining table dominates. I will go so far as to say you will never go into a French home – even the smallest flat, which doesn't have a dining-table. People sit together, chatting about their day and appreciating their food whilst eating. They eat slowly. This is the same at school. There are no packed lunches. The children eat a three-course meal all together, slowly.

Experts tell us that eating slowly gives time for the stomach to relate a 'full' message to the brain. Eat quickly and before the message gets to the brain, you've already eaten more than your body wants. And this is really what it's about. According to a joint French and American study in 2002, the biggest reason for the difference in obesity levels is, quite simply the amount of food eaten.

Over the last twenty years, people have thought it's to do with different diets which include or exclude categories of food; the Mediterranean diet – more olive oil not animal fats, the high meat content diet (Atkins) or the high carbohydrate diet (they noticed that the French have bread with all their meals).

The joint USA / French study came up with the staggeringly simple solution – the French eat less. And the study proved it. They compared portions served in restaurants and found that in the USA 25% more food is served per portion on average. Think of those pub meals in the UK. You are faced with an enormous oval plate with steak or gammon and chips piled high and hanging over. You are a big hero if you finish that.

Hot dogs are 63% bigger than in France and chocolate bars (e.g. Mars bars) are 41% bigger. Super-size is normal. Even if you succumb to a naughty but nice treat in France you would be eating less than in the UK and the USA. One of my young French university students just back from an assignment in London reported that the largest coke size in a French McDonald's is the smallest size in the UK.

So, the people serving us in restaurants and fast food outlets aren't helping us. Nor are the supermarkets in the UK who sell ready-made meals for two which in France would be for three or four. Even the recipes in France give smaller amounts. Over time, the French consume fewer calories and deadly heart disease is a lot lower – despite them having higher cholesterol levels (viz. the fatty delicacies and the sugary *pâtisseries*).

A French person has it much easier. She doesn't have to be the strong one, the one to say no, refuse to finish her food. She is served less, buys less in ready-made meals, makes less when following her recipes and would be stared at if she 'grazed' in the street, at her desk or even in the cinema.

I am just making my way out of the LeClerc supermarket where I have been writing this and noted that at the checkout, chocolate bars are scarce, but there is loads of chewing gum in multiple flavours shapes and packages – that must tell us something too.

Either we can all learn from these healthy customs, or we'll see France influenced by the rest of the west and their eating habits will go pear-shaped like us.

A woman eating alone is no strange thing

Dry bread is a typical snack for a French child

13. A Visit To Marseille
December 2008 / January 2009

At the end of summer we set off for a week in Marseille. There were plenty of reasons to go: It's in Provence so the weather stays warm long after Normandy is experiencing the first frosts of autumn, it's the second biggest city in France, and when you live in the countryside you don't want visits to more countryside, you want to see the big cities. But Marseille (the French spell it without a final 's', as they do with Lyon) is a long way away – some 800 kilometres and we didn't fancy driving. Then, the unexpected happened. Our bank came to our rescue. That doesn't seem quite right - doesn't someone have to rescue them these days?

I'm not great at loyalty cards and in fact I have been at cutting-up point several times in the past, but when the bank statement came through in August, there was a sentence telling us we had 2000 points each on our *S'miles* cards. *S'miles* cards are just another loyalty card, run by a group of companies including the SNCF – the French railways. This number of points, it said, entitled us to a return journey anywhere in France. Well, to cut a long story short, and although I was nearly cutting my wrists after hours on the phone, the tickets eventually arrived in the post. Yes, free rail tickets right from our home town to Marseille. We had to go.

A journey that would have taken 11 hours' driving, even by motorway (not forgetting the motorway fees and the cost of petrol), took 4 ½ hours by train. From Paris it was 3 hours to the minute on the high speed train which did not stop once before Marseille. So we stepped off the train into the mid-afternoon sun and a temperature of 29 degrees.

By the time we had wheeled our bags to the hotel (with an air-conditioned room, thankfully) we had personal experience of how friendly the natives are. People stopped us to ask which hotel we were looking for, advised us politely not to leave our backpack on a bench without keeping hold and told us what we really had to see in Marseille.

I said that Marseille is the second largest city in France, but it is also the oldest town in France. Greek sailors started using the port around 600 BC and called it Massalia. The Romans later took it over but it only began to expand as a city in the eleventh century.

One product they began to make around then, largely because the necessary ingredients are found locally, is soap. Its perfume floats out of all the back-street shops. Since someone told me about it soon after our arrival in France, I use it in liquid form, without any other product, in the washing machine. You don't need fabric softener and the natural smell is so good, people remark on it. *Savon de Marseille* is a totally natural product made from vegetable oils (72%) and is 100% biodegradable. It is also excellent for your skin (you can buy it in oil form to use as a moisturiser).

I don't know when the gypsies arrived, but they are still there, all around the area, playing their dark, romantic looks for all they are worth. You see them mostly in the evenings, because in the evenings, the heat has cooled a little and everyone takes to the streets. No-one wants to go inside to eat and so the restaurants weave their webs over the cobbled streets and the fountain squares to attract the tourist flies. The aroma of their specialities such as *Bouillabaisse* (fish soup), *coquilles St Jacques* (scallops) and mussels simmered in white wine permeates the warm air. Hovering on the edge of each web are the gypsy guitarists, singers and mandolin players, vying with the piped music from inside or each other outside. It's so romantic and so easy to take an interest in the musician and his music but he will clock any look or gesture and come in for the kill. It's fine to pay for your entertainment but sometimes the musicianship leaves a lot to be desired. Those wailing heartfelt throbs don't have the same effect three tones out of tune. One night, the restaurant manager himself came out to shoo the player away, so bad was he.

More difficult to cope with are the gypsy ladies who are not content with hogging a street corner to ask for alms. They approach you at your table. One lady dining on her own was approached by a gypsy lady with a baby, asking for food and the gypsy actually took some cake from her plate. The diner was very upset at this infringement of her privacy and went inside the restaurant to finish her meal.

I once did a study on the gypsies of Provence, because the gypsies gather each year at Saintes-Maries-de-la-Mer, not far from Marseille, to hold colourful processions and honour their local saint. It turns out gypsies got this name because people thought they came from Egypt. Other nomads were called Romanies because they were thought to come from Romania. However, it is now widely accepted that all these travelling people from the East originated in northern India and travelled for at least 1000 years westwards. When they came to the Mediterranean Sea, some went north to go west, via Romania and others went south via Egypt and through to Spain and France. They still have their own distinctive culture, music and dress although they have been in Provence for centuries.

The gypsies introduced tarot cards to France in the Middle-Ages. Card-playing became such an obsession (especially with the monks, apparently) that in 1369 a royal decree prohibited playing cards throughout the whole of France. Naturally, the decree had precisely the opposite effect and card-playing became even more popular. Marseille became the centre for the production of tarot playing cards.

Hopefully the inmates of the infamous prison, *Le Château d'If*, were allowed to play cards whilst incarcerated on the grim, forbidding island just outside the bay of Marseille. It makes a wonderful visit today and anyone who has read or seen The Count of Monte Christo will immediately conjure up Richard Chamberlain, hunched in a stone cell chipping away at the wall for fourteen years before his fantastic escape in a dead man's sack. In reality, nobody ever escaped the island and you can understand why when the guide shows you the sheer cliff drops into the sea, and explains that the sea is notoriously rough in the bay and anyway, most people couldn't swim in the nineteenth century. Nevertheless, it's a supremely romantic place in a fabulous setting.

When you look back at the harbour and the city from the Château d'If, a glint of gold above the horizon beckons. It's a long and arduous climb up the city streets, through a park and up to the cliff top by way of some 300 steps, but it's well worth the effort. The church at the top, called Notre Dame de la Garde was only built in the nineteenth century but there has been a chapel there to watch over seafarers since the Middle-Ages. The gold you see glistening from afar is a gilded statue of the Virgin and Child on the very top of the church standing 37 feet above the bell tower of the church. The real reason for the climb however, is the view over the whole of the city, the harbour and the islands at the mouth of the bay. Looking out at all that, you don't doubt the patriotism felt by the French for their beautiful country, here in the birthplace of the national anthem, dubbed 'The Marseillaise' because it was sung by revolutionary volunteers from Marseille. No wonder Glasgow seized the opportunity to be twinned with this city.

An idyllic few days away in an almost exotic location were almost over, when we were dawdling back to the hotel after a superb pizza on the fountain square. We stopped to look in a shop window and I lingered a few seconds longer than my husband, Eric. In the space of ten eerily silent seconds, my bag-strap eased itself from my shoulder and snapped down on my upper arm – so hard, my brain snapped into action. It wasn't me doing it!

Someone else was doing this and was now silently dragging at the strap from behind me. And just as silently I hung on. I have no idea why I didn't scream. It was instinct pure and simple. I hung on for dear life and the anger rose in my throat at the idea of someone stealing my stuff. The strap was dragged across the pavement with me behind it. I staggered and my foot twisted under me as I fell in the gutter. Eric had heard something now and turned, shouting at the Darth Vader figure yanking at my bag and making for the pillion seat of a scooter waiting in the road.

'Hang on, Viv!' Eric shouted. His words had the opposite effect. I couldn't have Eric running after two young thugs after his heart attack and a hip replacement.

So they got away and probably got no more than €30 cash from the bag. We had to undergo three hours in the police station. This was a surprising experience. The very central police station in Marseille on a Saturday night could only throw up three people in some sort of trouble. You would have thought it would be bursting at the seams. Once inside, the police were kind enough but very laid back. The female officer at the front desk stopped to talk for at least three minutes to her toddler at home before asking us to wait our turn for the formal procedure. 'You should stop your credit cards right away,' she advised.
'Yes, of course. Is there a phone we can use?'
'Sorry. There isn't a public payphone I'm afraid.' What? A victim couldn't ring home or to a friend for help? The police officer did look sheepish, but it didn't prevent us having to walk up the centre of town looking for a public phone.

There was a phone shop – a new-fangled replacement for the payphone- with booths inside. You pay the man at the desk after your calls. To cancel my French bank card cost us €40 in phone calls. The English phone call was much cheaper but like banging my head on a brick wall. I was put through to a call-centre in India, whose computer couldn't recognise our post code (well, it's in France) so I asked her to transfer me to Barclay's in the UK. I ended up talking to a young man in the USA who also wanted to close the conversation when he couldn't trace our postcode on his computer. I lost my rag a bit told him it was his job to trace the card as I was reporting it stolen and if someone else used it, I wouldn't accept the debt. He found he could trace us after all.

Back at the police station, the other two clients waiting to report their problems were not through. It took two hours for us to be seen by the officer who recorded the details. One finger typing was all he could manage - a very pleasant chap, just slow. It was approaching midnight and my ankle was really hurting. 'Where did it happen?' he asked. We tried to explain then ventured, 'Have you got a plan of the city so that we can show you?' They hadn't. Bare walls everywhere. Not a street map, metro map, nothing. He had to ask his female colleague and she had to guess the name of the street to put down on the report. How do they track down criminals?

Eric asked to use a loo. 'Strictly speaking, it's not for the public, but you can have the key.' The cistern didn't flush. We were glad to be out of there.

It wasn't the crime itself. The kids on the scooters probably have little idea of the trouble they cause. So much of my life was in that bag that I was now a non-person: no passport (in the bag because it was needed the day before), no bank cards, no camera, no mobile phone, no prescription glasses, no driving licence, no health card giving me rights to be treated in France. In short, until I could replace all this, I had no identity. And this is important In France where you are asked to prove who you are much more than in the UK. That's why we had to stick it out in the police station, to get the report which is needed to stand instead of all my papers.

There was a final kick in the teeth from our insurer who told us that we were not insured. Quite logical really. The theft was not from the house, nor had we travelled by car. One good thing though, for some reason or other, we had left the train tickets in the hotel room. We could, and did, get home.

Like the song says, 'It's nice to go travelling, but it's so much nicer, yes it's so much nicer to come home'.

14 Mind Your Language
February / March 2009

When I was little, during the fifties, my grandma often used to say, 'San Fairy Ann' whilst shrugging her shoulders. I never knew who she was talking about and I don't think she knew either. Years later, when studying French I heard French people say, *'Ça ne fait rien'* and the centime dropped. It means, 'It doesn't matter' and was a phrase brought back by soldiers in northern France during the First World War - along with 'wipers' for Ypres, 'eat-apples' for Étaples and a taste for Benedictine. I say the First World War because, after the Normandy landings in 1944, the soldiers were not around long enough to pick up the lingo. Apparently, in around 1920, a group of ex-soldiers in Hampshire started a cycling club and couldn't agree what to call it. One young chap shrugged his shoulders and said 'San Fairy Ann'. That cycling club is still pedalling today and carries the motto on its badge.

So ingrained in our habits are French phrases and expressions, that we rarely stop to wonder how they got there. When William conquered us, the French language came into use in England but mainly amongst the upper classes (since they were the French who were given land by the king).

Here's one story which illustrates this. In France, there is only one word for an animal and the meat that comes from it - *bœuf*, *porc* and *mouton*. In English there is a different word for the animal (cow, pig or sheep) and the meat from them. That's because those French nobles (De lacy, de

Houghton et al) were only concerned with domestic animals when presented as food on the platter in the great hall, so the French words became the words for the meats: beef, pork and mutton. The lower classes, the Anglo-Saxons (i.e. the rest of us) were the ones working with the animals and kept the old English names. Of course, the Anglo-Saxons didn't get to eat much of the meat they only used the words to describe the live animals.

To this day, there is something affected about using French phrases such as *c'est la vie* or, *je ne sais pas* and we always feel we have to use them with an ironic smile as though to say, 'I know I'm putting on airs and graces, but I'm not really like that.' I suppose the ultimate joke of this sort would be Sybil Fawlty's 'Pretentious? Moi?'

The French have adopted English vocabulary too - despite the attempts of the *Académie Française*. This august body has the hapless task of preserving the purity of the French language and defending its position as an international language in the face of English (or American) infiltration. Most memorably, they insisted on banning *le weekend* and using *la fin de semaine* instead. Needless to say, the ban didn't last long. However, whereas we Brits feel rather self-conscious using French words, the French just think, after a decent interval, that the new words have always been French. If you ask a French person about words such as *sandwich, cool, le fast-food* and all sports' names apart from *tennis and lacrosse,* they will be sure they are French words. They even 'frenchify' new words. For example, they have not only adopted *email,* but they have made it into a French verb – *emailer.*

For us, anything different or exotic attracts the adjective, 'French'. Look up 'French' in a dictionary and you will find French bread, French polish, French windows, French dressing. You can understand why – the object would have been different and exotic to our minds and the nearest different land is France, so we called it French.

On the other hand, most French phrases with *à l'anglaise* (in the English manner) denote something banal and uninteresting: *pommes à l'anglaise* are potatoes boiled in salt water, *crème anglaise* is plain old custard, *une assiette anglaise* is a plate of cold meat, and *un jardin à l'anglaise* has been left to nature. Napoleon thought of us 'a nation of shopkeepers' and Voltaire said that 'the English have sixty religions but only one sauce'.

In English, the adjective, 'French' takes on a different quality with 'French kissing', 'French knickers' and 'French lessons' – not just exotic but erotic too. We obviously think the French are sexier than we are – put 'French' in front of anything and I think we all appreciate the nuance it gives – (think of 'French letters'). Whether in fact the French are more erotic / interested in sex than we are I cannot say. It's one hypothesis I have never been able to prove, being a boring Brit and a married woman for thirty years. However, the only time in my life I was asked to have an affair was by a Frenchman – on the first meeting at a respectable gathering in a French town hall. He was decorum itself when I blushed and stammered *'Non, merci'*. My husband and I were invited (at the same gathering) to his home where we met his elegant and charming wife. Still, one swallow doesn't make a summer. What is true is that, when the sexually-contracted disease, syphilis, came to England, it was called 'The French Pox'.

That maybe simply a convenient insult, and both nations are guilty of that. There was a very popular French film in the sixties about some teenage boys coming to England and picking up every English girl in sight. It was called *'A Nous les Petites Anglaises'* and that phrase is now a by-word for 'easy' English girls.

You might be surprised to learn that if we have nick-named condoms 'French letters', the French have turned the joke back on us by calling them *les capotes anglaises*. (In fact, the condom was named after a Frenchman and there is a town in France of this name).

More worryingly, if we think the French are risqué in an enviable way, their view of English sexual habits is rather tainted by *le vice anglais* – homosexuality (I guess this is a side-effect of our single-sex public school system which doesn't exist in France). There is also a verb *anglaiser* which means to act like an Englishman in matters of money, i.e. to swindle or to cheat.

Of course, our envy of their sexiness and their envy of our royal family has given rise to mutual insults over the years. They are envious of the Royal family because they no longer have one of their own. They also adore all those horsey country Barbour and Mulberry clothes. So, when we talk about taking 'French leave' we are implying the French are sneaky or cowardly. They have done a tit for tat on this one and express the same idea in *filer à l'anglaise* (to sneak away like the English). We call them frogs (most likely because frogs' legs are traditional fare) but they get their own back by calling us *les rosbifs* after our traditional dish.

So insults have been flung across the English Channel - why is it called the English Channel anyway, when it separates two countries? Their Norman duke killed our king Harold and took over our country in the eleventh century. Then we English invaded and occupied bits of north-western France during the Hundred Years War. There are villages near us called *Anglesqueville, Englesqueville* and *Saint Marie aux Anglais* because English troops were stationed there in the thirteenth and fourteenth centuries. The French still bring up the spectre of Joan of Arc, blaming us for burning her at the stake. This is usually said with a laugh, rather like an English person asking a Frenchman if businessmen send their wives to the country with the children in summer so they can spend more time with the mistress. They are both waiting for a reaction. It rarely fails.

There was, in the last century, a backlash against the pretentiousness of using French when there are perfectly good English words. This was promulgated by Nancy Mitford in the Fifties. The idea was that you could tell a real upper-crust person by the vocabulary they use. 'U' and 'Non-U' were the terms used for 'upper-class' and 'not upper-class' and generally the 'U' version is straightforward and English rather than pretentious and French. So, it is 'U' to use 'lavatory', 'napkin', 'what?' and 'graveyard', rather than 'toilet', 'serviette', 'pardon?', and 'cemetery'. It is a bit of nonsense really because 'napkin' for example, is from the French *nappe* anyway, and means 'a little tablecloth' and 'lavatory' is from Latin which is at the root of both languages.

On the subject of lavatories, our modern term 'loo' is interesting as that too, comes from the French. In the seventeenth and eighteenth centuries French was used in

Scotland because of the 'Auld Alliance' between the two countries. Chamber-maids would shout from the overhanging upstairs windows 'Gardez-vous de l'eau!' before emptying chamber pots into the street. The name 'gardyloo' is still used in Edinburgh to mean lavatory, and 'loo' has become the term used by the middle-classes all over Britain.

For the worst of all insults, you cannot do better than the two fingers 'Up yours, Delors!' (as *The Sun* had it). I have always thought it was throbbing with sexual connotations (although I could never think what the two fingers symbolised). Never mind that Winston Churchill used it to signify victory. He turned his palm outwards – not the same thing at all, although some people have said he knew it was a double-edged sword.

Well, a few years ago, we visited the museum at Azincourt in Normandy, scene of the famous 1415 battle (before we burnt Joan of Arc) between Henry V of England and Charles VI of France. And in that museum is told the story of the two-fingered salute.

It was the use of the longbow used by the English, rather than the crossbow used by the French which was the deciding factor in the battle. This is because a longbow could be loaded from the quiver on the bowman's back and fired with much greater speed than the crossbow could, The English longbow men were formidable. So, when the French soldiers captured an English archer, and as prisoners were not usually killed but returned after the fight, they took to chopping off the index and middle fingers of his right hand before they sent him back to the other side. This made the bowman useless as he could no longer draw back the bowstring. Consequently, the longbow men on the English side took to thrusting their two fingers in the air at the French as a gesture of defiance. (I've still got my two fingers! Na na, na-na na!).

Now, it is gracious of the French to present this story in their museum at all, considering it doesn't show them in such a good light, and remembering that the two fingered gesture is not used in other countries, these are two good reasons why I am persuaded that this is indeed the origin of the two-fingers' salute.

Of all foreign cultures, French has had the most influence on the British and it shows in both languages. We just both hate to admit it - which is a damn shame. Pardon my French.

15 La Crise Économique
April / May 2009

Yes it's official now. We've gone from 'a down-turn in the economy', through a 'crisis' and now to the longer-lasting recession. Even the word 'depression' has slipped from the chancellor's lips.

But hang-on, I'm writing from France whose banks are much more solid and whose property is still much cheaper than in England. How can there be a recession here?

After all, French people have never been able to borrow more than 3.3 times their income to buy a house or have a loan of more than 80% of the value of the property. Borrowers have to prove their salary is dependable too. Although house prices have risen slowly over the past ten years, it has not been at the galloping rate seen in the UK.

That's why there is no credit-crunch here in France because there never was a credit free-for-all. No sub-prime mortgages or over-lending. French people have not re-mortgaged. They usually don't use credit cards for purchases – they use debit cards, which means the money goes directly out of your account and if your account hasn't the money or an agreed overdraft, your purchase will not go through.

So why is France suffering at all?

Well, here, it's been less sudden but wages have stagnated for the past five years, manufacturing jobs have been lost -

the car industry alone accounts for 10% of the manufacturing base - and the cost of living has been quietly rising due to world market prices. Basically, it's a global thing. Nobody escapes. Because the level of spending by the UK and The USA has plummeted, French exports (along with Japan and all other exporting countries) have suffered.

Here, the situation is called *la crise économique* and people are certainly tightening their belts. *Le Monde* newspaper reported on those middle-income families who once were comfortably-off and who now only manage to get to the end of the month by eating meat once a week instead of every day, cutting down on paid leisure activities for themselves and the children, and by wives buying fewer clothes. In fact some wives are swapping their clothes with their friends instead and they also have their clothes altered at the dressmaker's when they begin to look old-fashioned.

The clothes shops are getting desperate discounting up to 75% and even splashing *soldes de crise* (recession sales) over the shop windows but to little effect.

And yet, I was at my hairdresser's last week and asked them if trade has slackened off. They assured me they were busier than this time last year. After some discussion, they concluded that for most French women, having their hair done is essential and for others a consolation when they can't buy new clothes. This bit of investigative research rebounded on me I'm afraid. I was so keen to get them all talking honestly about things that I opted for those silly extras they put on after the shampoo, and bought products for 'volume' and 'gloss' to use at home. Result: the bill was €99 compared to €60 something.

I am seeing more people toting Aldi, Lidl and Ed plastic bags recently. So these bags are evidence that people are shopping at the cheaper supermarkets. It seems it's almost a statement of the new 'make-do chic'. I even heard somebody referring to *Système D* which harks back to the last war and means *Système Débrouillard*. This is like our own war-time slogan 'make-do and mend'. My favourite is 'ED' – not a nerd's name but initials for European Distribution. Most people don't realise that ED is run by the big Carrefour group. It's just a collection of own-brand products mixed with a few other brands. The choice is limited and there are very few non-food goods (all the better to keep impulse-buying at bay), but at least the stock is properly displayed on shelves and not piled up haphazardly in cardboard boxes.

Naturally the French continue to top up the supermarket run with trips to the butcher for quality fresh meat, the market for fresh vegetables and fruit and the baker for fresh bread. They still have their traditions and buy a lot fewer ready-made meals than we do. Having mentioned the baker, it's also true to say that the bread-baking machine is a big hit here. Not only can you save money, but you avoid the problem of your *baguettes* going stale before the day is out.

Holidays abroad are going out of the window – although when you have a country the size of France with such a variety of landscapes and climates, it's not difficult to go somewhere different without going abroad. There is usually some member of the family who has a second home in Brittany or in the south and the French have a tradition of holidays in August with the extended family – if not at the grandparents' farm, then at a camp-site in mobile homes or caravans.

So people are feeling the pinch quite a bit and they don't consider the government's actions to stimulate the economy are helping them either. That's why there was a one-day general strike on 28th January. As usual, the biggest supporters were the public workers. Teachers, transport workers, post-office employees were in the front line expressing their disgust at President Sarkozy giving taxpayers' money to the banks and the car industry when nobody seems to be directly helping the workers. Sounds familiar?

The English ex-pats living here have the same problems as the French and something else as well. The great majority are not in regular jobs here. Most of us are retired and have completed our working lives in the U.K. Our pensions are paid in sterling. In six short months, the pound has lost 30% of its value. Say your pensions added up to £18,000 per year, that sum was translated into roughly €27,000. Now, in February 2009 as I write, the same sum transfers into €18,000.

We fall into this category but for us it is a bit mitigated. Last year I was sixty and got two small pensions. Small because I didn't work the full 40 years necessary (a fate that befalls most of us wives and mothers). It took us a few months to realise we were not benefitting from the extra pensions. All of it had been eaten up by the poor exchange rate. A lot of people are worse off than we are though. If you calculated you would just have enough to live on before last year, you are really suffering now.

It's the same for those Brits who run bed and breakfast or *gîtes*. If their customers are Brits either they will pay in pounds which are worth less now, or there will be fewer of them coming over for holidays as they don't want to pay in Euros.

And it's the fall in the pound that has made a huge difference. It means that, for the first time in twenty years, petrol is actually cheaper in England than in France. It means that Brittany Ferries are running day trips – not to France for cheap cigarettes and alcohol, but from France to England for clothes shopping trips. So, are the Brits migrating en masse back to Blighty? The estate agents' magazines report that there are hardly any Britons coming to France now. The removal firms report very little work moving people in either direction. This is understandable. France is much less attractive with the pound at such a low ebb and Brits are much less likely to have spare money to buy a second home or confidence in their income level to move here permanently.

That doesn't mean however, that the Brits are going back, it just means fewer are coming out here. There are some Brits going back to the UK – as always. There is always a percentage who go back – usually within two years of living here but it hasn't gone up much because of the economic crisis. The reasons for people going back have been identified as mainly; family needs (for example aged parents needing help in the UK, teenage children not settling in the new country) or because it has been much more difficult than they imagined to earn a living here.

We personally know four English couples who are hoping to go back to the UK -actually one of those couples has now sold and is not too unhappy at the price they've got for their house given that they will get virtually £1 for €1. None of these couples are going back because of the recession. One couple is giving up their second home here because of ill-health (two houses to maintain have become too much), two couples are moving back to be near grandchildren born since they came out here and in the case of the other couple, the wife had not realised how quiet and depressing the countryside can be in winter.

For Eric and me, our French adventure is by no means over so we are not thinking of going back to the UK, but the shrinking income from our pensions is making some changes.

On the micro level, I have got out some old 1950s recipe books and now, with one chicken for €5, I do a chicken with bacon and cider meal for four, then pick the pieces of meat left on the carcass and make a chicken, mushroom and gravy pie, and finally simmer up the carcass to make cream of chicken soup.

Since Christmas, we have decided to write down everything we spend on a sheet of paper. That simple action has made us cut down dramatically on trivial spending. So, although we continue to frequently invite friends for a meal, I now start by looking at what foodstuffs are in the pantry and the freezer and working out a menu from there, rather than going out and spending an extra €80.

Unfortunately, I rebelled against the vegetable garden two years ago because of a bad back and I'm regretting it now. We also have a regime of paying for electricity (everything is electric in this house) which means cheaper electricity except for 21 days a year. Of course these 21 days are in winter so on those days we don't use the central heating and it's back to war-time living.

On the macro level, we have indeed begun to think of moving. It's to do with age and the shrinking income. The amount of land with this house is too much to maintain and I know that the next move should be to a village or small town with shops and amenities.

Eric has played a wild card by suggesting we look at somewhere warmer like the Mediterranean coast near Narbonne in the south-west. This area is much cheaper than the Riviera and doesn't have an extreme hot / cold climate like the interior of France. We are going to have a week's holiday down there in spring to have a look around. I'm trying to be thrilled about it but my stomach drops when I think of it. I know I would miss this part of Normandy so much: the people are similar to us, northerners – friendly and open and of course the half-timbered houses and the gently-rolling landscape is so picturesque. Maybe the recession will be over soon, then I won't have to think about it.

16 Pets Or Pests
May / June 2009

It is idyllic. The sun is shining onto the verdant fields, cows grazing contentedly under the apple trees, flicking their tails lazily over their backs and looking at us with their brown and white bespectacled faces. Despite the sun and the effort making me sweat, I am thinking, 'This is what we came to France for'- a warm and sunny unspoilt country panorama. Well, not completely unspoilt; the effort of pedalling up the hill and listening to Eric chivvy me along, 'come on, Viv. Keep pedalling,' or 'Keep going, Viv. The view from up here is gorgeous' is really annoying. Especially when I do eventually catch him up and start to get my breath back, he sets set off again straight away, since he has had five minutes rest waiting for me. He always does that. I end up mentally throwing daggers at his back from way down the slope.

Anyway, this particular day, only two months after moving in here, I had just rounded the last corner of the ride uphill, got off my bike and noticed a pristine white villa in its grounds on the right, with a long laurel hedge to keep trespassers out, when I heard it; a dog. Even though the gates were open, I foolishly assumed the dog would be used to people and would be a family pet like they are in England.

As I pushed my bike past the gates, the dog, a big black hairy monster that I discovered later to be a *Briard* (a mountain dog), came hurtling out of the gates straight towards me and sank his teeth into my right thigh. And believe me, there is plenty to go at.

I wailed pathetically and managed to kick him off. Eric came back into view to tell me off for shouting in the peaceful countryside. I limped up the road to him and embarrassed him even more by pulling down my jogging pants to show him the damage. He was impressed. There were two sets of fang marks and a huge amount of blood and red leg.

The care given to me was fast and efficient. On that Saturday afternoon about 6 pm in the hospital in Lisieux, there was nobody waiting in emergency. A nurse and a doctor both saw me to dress the wound and give a tetanus injection. Then we were asked to go to the police station in our nearby village. The police knew the dog and informed the owners of the procedure they had to follow. That meant the owners going three times to the vet and having the copy of a certificate of clean health put in our letter-box.

The next day the owners came round with flowers and apologies. The lady did look distressed when she saw my leg, now black from my knee to my bottom, but she and her husband assured me their dog was gentleness itself with their three children. So when the police asked if I wished to complain formally, I demurred because it was the first offence. If I had, the policeman said it would have been destroyed. I did hesitate when the first copy of the clean health certificate came though. It said the dog's name was Macho. Do you really call a fluffy pet Macho?

Some months later, I went to visit the retired village schoolteacher. Her black Labrador-mix met me at the gates and walked with me to the house. Even under the watchful eye of his owner, this one bit me on the wrist before we got to the front door.

You see, this is the countryside and lots of French people have dogs. Only they're not pets in the way people have pets in England. These are guard dogs and their owners are proud to tell you so. They have a sign on the gate saying '*Chien méchant*' (literally 'bad dog') or how about the notice in one picture I have seen? It reads, 'This dog can make it from its kennel to the gate in four and a half seconds. If you can't do better than that, you'd better stay where you are'. I do not really know why the people round here are so protective of their property. Burglary is quite rare and anyway, most of our country folks' houses haven't much worth stealing. I mean, they are hardly stuffed with home cinemas and blackberries (well, not the electronic sort). It's just an attitude that goes back a long way. This is my property and you'd better stay out.

Yes, French people have animals. In fact there are around 17 dogs to every hundred people in France, one of the highest ratios in the world and France has the most pets of all European countries. 45% of French homes have both a cat and a dog. The fact is though, they are mostly kept for practical reasons: to guard the property, to kill vermin, or to be eaten.

It is significant that there is no single French word for 'pet', merely *animal familier* or *animal domestique*. My students smile behind their hand when I tell them my husband calls me his pet. They think this is insulting and would rather call their dearest 'my cabbage'.

So, in the countryside, the animals are usually kept outside, sometimes in a pen and sometimes chained up. It's rare to see French people walking their dogs in the countryside. All country people are not necessarily farmers but they mostly have a dog (to guard the house), a cat (to kill mice and rats), some chickens (for eggs and their meat) a couple of sheep (to keep the grass down and for meat) or a couple of pigs (for meat). Our neighbour, the baker, has two donkeys in his field. They are to keep the grass down and amuse the children who come out on school trips to visit his rustic bakery.

In our first year here, we were walking round the village with our daughters and they were delighted to see a bank of cages containing lovely, fluffy rabbits, against the outside wall of a dilapidated cottage. They were not so delighted when we told them they were going to be killed to eat, though. You don't have to call the local abattoir to come and do the dirty for rabbits. Apparently, your grandmother takes the rabbit by the ears and whacks it on the back of its neck (from where we get the term 'rabbit punch' I suppose), then takes a pointed stick to poke its eyes out. This is to let all the blood from the meat. Nice hey?

I do agree we townies, especially in England have lost connection with real country life and if we eat meat we should face up to where it comes from. It's just that there is meat and meat. We English just can't face up to horse meat and when, on one occasion, we found out the huge sausage we had been given was made from donkey meat, we couldn't face that either. Frogs' legs ditto. For further amusement, you can visit snail farms to watch them breed – and take a picnic too. You sometimes see old couples out picking slimy snails from the roadside for lunch.

Being so in your face with animals as food, you can imagine hunting is very popular. There's another country-walk danger. The quiet of a Sunday morning in the midst of a landscape picture is punctured by the noise of guns. These are not horse-riding hunters because horse-riding is an expensive sport, more exclusive even than in England. These hunters are walkers armed with shotguns. I hear them as I hang out the washing and hope they are reasonable shots. Shooting is considered almost a citizens' right here. That's because a lot of land belongs to the Republic and therefore every citizen has a right to use it, gather wood in it and shoot animals in it - unlike England where the majority of land is privately owned. They have the French revolution to thank for that.

One business man I taught some years ago would bring me a plastic bag with a dead pheasant or partridge as an offering, thinking it a normal, polite thing to do. Even fishermen here don't throw back the fish they catch. They will always eat what they catch, thank you very much.

If animals are kept for practical reasons and they are part of the natural world, it stands to reason that what they do naturally is – well, natural. The French are notorious for just letting their dogs out to relieve themselves anywhere. The authorities do put up lots of signs and provide plastic bags but the French don't scoop, their dogs just poop. They ignore the 'no dogs allowed on the beach' signs and you have to watch your step on any town pavement.

Last year, we had to change our venue for our ladies' book club. We used to meet in a very convenient cafe in town where we were welcome to sit for hours with one coffee. There was no loud music so we could talk and the proprietor was very friendly. But he has two dogs – no doubt to guard the place at night. These dogs roamed the cafe all the time and one day pooped right under our table. The ladies (all English) couldn't put up with this, yet we felt we couldn't say anything to the owner. We didn't think he would understand. After all, it's only natural to poo and widdle, isn't it? Even the men in France simply stop at the roadside and pee at the side of their car when they feel the need (and say *bonjour* to you if you pass by), so what hope is there of refining their dogs' manners?

Maybe all this makes it a little more understandable why the French cosmetic industry is one of the last remaining in Europe to be using animals for testing purposes. Companies such as L'Oreal contribute millions of Euros to the French economy. Despite a near-total ban on animal testing for cosmetics from 2009, L'Oreal has quietly launched a legal action aimed at stopping the ban.

And yet, in the towns there is a totally opposite phenomenon. Here, the dog exists as a fashion accessory. It is necessarily small and is more often carried than walked. It can fit into a designer bag and is usually a poodle or a shiatsu in a fetching little jacket. When this elegant pet-owner takes the dog out, it's for show and you are meant to stop and admire the pooch as you would a new baby in a pram.

Although food shops make an effort to bar pets, it isn't unusual to see a supermarket trolley containing a dog or two. The elegant owner isn't going to be turned away. And because these owners are usually well-heeled, most restaurants allow dogs. Mostly they lie unnoticed under their owner's table, but occasionally have been seen sitting on a chair and being served like any other customer.

French hotels charge a rate (about €8 a night) for pets and there is no discrimination against pets when renting accommodation. There are certainly more pet grooming shops in France than in Britain.

Last year, the former French President Francois Mitterrand was rushed to hospital after being badly bitten by his white Maltese poodle. Apparently the little mite was being treated for depression and became increasingly prone to making vicious attacks, despite being treated with anti-depressants.

Whichever way you look at it, it's a dog's life in France.

P.S. I am told that in the South-East, around Narbonne, there is a constant wind from the mountains. Communications to Geneva, where my daughter lives, is not good, and all the houses I have seen on the internet look suburban and characterless. Even in the recession, Normandy is home in France for me.

CE CHIEN COUVRE LA DISTANCE NICHE → PORTAIL EN 4 SECONDES ½ SI VOUS N'EN FAITES PAS AUTANT, RESTEZ DONC OÙ VOUS ÊTES...

Would you dare ignore our neighbour's warning?

Rabbits are not for sale as pets at Lisieux market

17 Ken's War
August / September 2009

One lunch-time in early June in the small town of Pont L'Evêque, I was killing time in a café before going to teach my next English lesson in a biscuit factory. Out of the blue, I heard the dulcet tones of a Lancashire accent from the next table. An elderly couple were discussing what to order.

'Do you think the waiter will speak English? I only want something simple like a ham sandwich... I wonder what this lady on the next table is having.'

I butted in out of nosiness of course. I just had to find out where they were from, so I helped them order a ham sandwich and a *croque-monsieur*. To my delight, Mr Oldham said he was from Unsworth near Bury (my husband went to school near there). To my amazement, he said he was 89 years old and had driven all the way from Unsworth. And then, to my satisfaction, I guessed correctly that he was here for the 65th Normandy Landing commemorations.

The month before that, the Prime Minister had said the occasion would be a 'non-event' and the Queen would not be attending. It was never clear whether the Queen had received an invitation from Président Sarkozy or not, but there was an outcry from the public and at the last minute it was announced that Prince Charles would be standing in for the Queen. At the ceremony in Arromanches, Gordon Brown was actually booed. He had not appreciated that so few veterans are left, that this year the 65th anniversary would mark the transition between living memory and history.

We were there at Pegasus Bridge, having met up again with Kenneth Oldham, from Unsworth, and his friend Joyce Mason. The atmosphere was friendly, and very moving. Scots pipers and veterans processed across the bridge, the Café Gondrée was doing a roaring trade, The Café Gondrée, the first building to be freed from the German occupation, has hardly changed since 1944 apart from being festooned with photos and best wishes from the war-time famous like Richard Todd who surely must be the only person to have served in the real battle and then starred in its film 'The Longest Day'?

After our chance meeting in Pont L'Eveque, I had rummaged through my old copies of Northern Life to find the article I wrote in 2007 about the Landings. For that article I had done a bit of research and found that soldiers from Lancashire had been in the first landings near Ranville and Pegasus Bridge. Kenneth had just mentioned that he had served in the 13th Lancashire Parachute Battalion, the very regiment I had written about. So, at Pegasus Bridge and over lunch at our house a few days later, Ken took the trouble to tell me some of his war-time memories.

Kenneth joined up at the age of twenty with the 13th South Lancashire Regiment in 1940, after working as an apprentice electrician and boot-maker. He started training at Ringway (the present Manchester airport site), moved on to Cheltenham where he met Harry Green who was from Northampton and who became his best mate, then together they moved on to Larkhill barracks, Wiltshire.

By that time, the military strategists had realised they needed parachute regiments for the first time ever, as in the First World War there were none- (The UK's first airborne assault took place on 10 February 1941 in Italy.) Consequently, eight hundred or so soldiers were assembled in the gym at Larkhill and the Commanding Officer Lt. Col. Peter Luard gave the news that they were no longer the South Lancashire Regiment but the 13th Parachute Battalion.

'You are all volunteers!' he proclaimed, 'and anyone who doesn't wish to be a volunteer has to see me on company orders at 3pm!' Two men resisted as conscientious objectors but both served in the medical corps and indeed both ended up with the MM for bravery.

In the anxious days before D-day, there were suspicions of Germans dropping spies and terrorist attackers into the south of England. Kenneth and Harry were sent out with others digging trenches around Salisbury plain. Harry was working with a pick and Kenneth was shovelling the earth away. As luck would have it, Harry caught Kenneth on the hand with his pick and Kenneth had to be treated in hospital and missed the first wave of gliders and boats into Normandy. He followed two or three days later in an old reclaimed Belgian boat called The Leopoldville, with a group of eight men and a captain, who proclaimed, 'Right boys, we're off tomorrow. I'm coming back and so are you!'

Their battalion had taken the village of Ranville, just next to Pegasus Bridge after a bloody fight and Kenneth discovered that his mate Harry Green had been killed. Harry had been in a slit trench by the side of a wall in the village and a mortar bomb had hit the wall and killed him.

Kenneth was keen to explain to me that not all the soldiers in the parachute regiments are dropped into the war zone by parachute. A parachute operation is no good unless there is immediate support. 'That was the trouble at Arnhem' said Kenneth.

Like every other regiment the Paras need back-up services and Kenneth, due to the pre-war jobs he had done, was the equipment-repairer, the soldier to see to get your kit repaired, and generally - speaking, Kenneth was not fazed by his comrades' requests. He was taken aback, however when one day, before leaving for Normandy, Captain Spencer Daisley took him aside and explained that he had had a testicle removed as a result of a war wound and he was anxious not to lose the other, so could Ken make him a protective shield for it? Yes, he could. Ken made a jim-dandy one made of fine leather.

Captain Daisley sadly died on the first landing mission. The plane pulling his glider was shot down but managed to release the glider which landed some 18 miles off course, to the east of Caen. There were six or seven men aboard who survived the landing but who were met and outnumbered by the Germans. The graves marked with the names of those who died in that glider, are at a village called Saint Vaast-en-Auge, just inland from Houlgate. The mayor's son in that village, much later bought the old *mairie* and made it into a tiny museum dedicated entirely to those men.

The saddest duty and the one that most affected Kenneth, was burial duty. After Ranville was liberated, there were hundreds of dead soldiers to be buried. The bodies were piled up above ground, each one wrapped in his gas-cape and with his face covered so that the grave-diggers did not have to see them. But as they were laid into their grave, the grave-digger had to open the cape and remove the identity-disc for the records. It was when he saw the name of his sergeant, Sergeant Hughes, on the disc he had just pulled off that it got to him. Back at home, just before leaving for France, Kenneth had seen his own brother put to rest after dying of rheumatic fever. The comparison was stark. His brother had been washed and dressed and presented with dignity. These boys were still dirty and bloodied from battle, without any coffin, just dropped in the hole. Even worse, time was precious, and the troops had to press on towards Pont L'Eveque, the battles for the end of the war were only just beginning. Occasionally, the grave the soldiers dug for their comrades was slightly short for the soldier it was to contain. The grave-diggers had to push the body down with their spade or bend the legs to fit. After four days, Kenneth sought out the padre and asked to be taken off this duty.

Over two thousand British soldiers are interred at Ranville cemetery and a large proportion of those are from the 6th Airborne Division.

Moving on up the coast towards the next village, in a line, under the trees to stay out of sight as much as possible, Ken's company didn't fool an old French man who came across them. He excitedly waved a large bottle of transparent liquid in front of Kenneth, who was thirsty and drank in great gulps. He collapsed on the floor and thought he was poisoned. It wasn't water, it was Calvados and stronger than any whisky he had tasted before.

Slowly Kenneth's company fought their way up to Pont L'Eveque which proved to be a long and difficult battle, the last before the Seine and opening the way to Paris. There was heavy resistance from the Germans and after prolonged fighting without making headway into the town itself, the company were ordered to withdraw – never retreat, just withdraw, in order to advance again. The second assault was successful and soon after that, Kenneth and his regiment were taken back to England by boat for rest and recuperation before being sent over to Belgium in October 1944.

Two memories stand out in Kenneth's mind about Belgium and they are about how the soldiers lived when on campaigns. Kenneth and a few mates were told to find their own billets in a village. They knocked on a door and were invited in – the Belgians were most hospitable. However, the poverty in which this family lived astonished Kenneth. The flagstones on the floor were strewn with straw as bedding for the soldiers. The youngest children were put in open drawers in a huge sideboard to sleep. There was a huge tiled stove in the corner into which the father kept throwing logs and pushing them down into the fire with his bare hands. He turned to tell the soldiers about his stove. 'My son is in the resistance here in our village,' he said, 'and there was a German soldier in the occupying force, who made a nuisance of himself. He ended up in this stove chopped up into bits.'

Also in Belgium, they were billeted in a convent near Namur and Dinant, south of Brussels. Although the nuns had to take in thirty or forty men, which must have thoroughly upset their routine, they were, Kenneth recalls, magnificent. The army language was a bit rough but the men assumed the nuns wouldn't understand. There was a lot of swearing and joking going on whilst they cleaned their kit and prepared for the next-day's fighting. As they were leaving, one of the sisters came up to them. 'Good morning chaps,' she said in excellent English, 'I do hope things are not as bad as you obviously expect.'

During that same cleaning session the night before, one fellow started singing, 'Abide with Me'. They all jeered and shouted at him to shut to heck up but he insisted. 'Very likely, I'll be dead at this time tomorrow. I'm singing for my own funeral.' So he did, and he was - prophetically enough.

In the Ardennes, Kenneth says the hardest thing to contend with was the weather, as it was now deep winter. They were joined by the Guards Armoured regiment who had a reputation for toughness. Kenneth and his mates were told to cross a bridge into Germany but there were already some Americans on the scene who were going to blow up the bridge. There was a face-off between the Guards and the Americans. The guards announced, 'You are *not* going to blow up this bridge' and proceeded to cross it. No Americans were going to gainsay the Guards.

So Kenneth served, with welcome rests in England, all through the end of the war from Normandy to Germany and later was sent out to Java via India to serve there, where the Japs had just been ousted. The Javanese were so grateful for the arrival of the British that they stood in the gutter whenever they passed. The Javanese were also the poorest people Kenneth had ever met.

For the past fifteen years, since the fiftieth commemoration of the Landings in Normandy, Kenneth has been making the journey back to Pegasus Bridge and the beaches in June; first with his wife, who sadly died four years ago, and now with an old and loyal friend, Joyce.

On the sixtieth anniversary, Ken and Joyce wanted to come over to Normandy but couldn't find accommodation, so they went down to Portsmouth instead where there were some fine ceremonies and spectacles. A lady picked him out of the crowd and asked Ken if he would be interviewed by Harry Secombe. There were 10 000 people there and Ken wasn't keen to do it but she persisted and promised them a good seat. Little did he know that the occasion would be broadcast on national TV and his brother-in-law in Ontario would actually see him live on the screen.

Two years ago, Ken was once again in Normandy for the big occasion and visited the new museum at Pegasus Bridge. The English curator introduced Kenneth to another old soldier. 'Do you remember Jack Watson? He was a captain in your battalion.' The captain approached Kenneth and said, 'What do they call you?'
'They used to call me Ginger,' said Kenneth.
'I can't call you Ginger now,' said the captain, 'and by the way, don't call me Captain, call me Jack.'

What a war. What memories.

Kenneth will be coming over to Normandy for some years yet, I sincerely hope. I thank him for the pleasure and honour of meeting him and for trusting me with his memories. He would also be happy to be in contact with any other veterans from the 13th Parachute (South Lancashire) Regiment.

Ken in 1942 (aged 22)

18 To Your Very Good Health
October / November 2009

Picture the scene in an office: two people are making an arrangement. 'When would it be convenient for you?' asks the professional. The customer looks in her diary. 'In two weeks from now?'
'That's fine. Please see my secretary for the details.' What is surprising about this conversation is that it, or something like it, takes place, not in a business setting, but a doctor's surgery. On that occasion, he was an eminent neurosurgeon and I was the patient. But this is France and that means I was also the customer, so my wishes were important.

At no time during the last year have I been told to 'wait and see' or to go away and come back if it gets worse. I've had x-rays and an MRI scan and been to see a rheumatologist and a neurologist. And each specialist has discussed the matter with me as though I am an equal and included me in the decision process. Because, as a user of the French health service, I am a customer, not a humble recipient of government charity.

On the other hand, along with information comes responsibility. So when you have x-rays done, they are given to you, the customer and you are responsible for taking them with you to the specialist. Similarly with blood tests and the like. You are given all the information and you can see the score. It's a subtle but important difference between the UK and the French systems which means that you, the patient, are in fact the customer and you must take responsibility for your health. In England, whenever my husband had a blood test for cholesterol, he would ring the GP's surgery, and after about two weeks would be told by the receptionist that it was OK. He never saw his own results.

There is little waiting over here. You come out of the radiologist's with your x-rays under your arm. Your blood test arrives in the post at home the next day. Here's an example: Eric my husband, felt some chest pains and since he had a by-pass 17 years ago, he knew it was a little warning, so rang his cardiologist (without going through the GP, as he is an annual customer) and made an appointment for three days' time. The cardiologist said he should have a blood test before he came so Eric went the following morning to the laboratory for a blood test (no appointment needed). Two hours later, the laboratory rang our house to tell us there was something that needed attention and to go to the hospital straight away. We drove to the hospital where he was kept for a week and given the relevant tests; ECG and angiogram and was only sent home after they had adjusted his medication.

To back up our personal experiences and what our friends tell us, Paul Dutton, a historian at the University of Northern Arizona, has published a comparison of Health Care in the United States and France. His comparison is of great interest at the moment when Barrack Obama is trying to introduce a national health scheme. Paul Dutton concludes that, by following the French example, you can include all the population without sacrificing customer choice. Back in 2000, the World Health Organization ranked France as having the best health care in the world. Last year, another study was done on 19 industrialised nations and found that France came first again (judged to have the fewest deaths that could have been prevented with better health care).

Some of this is quite simply because there are far more doctors in France than in any other European country. As a result, health care costs a lot and France is in debt because of it. The government has a hard job to try to reduce the debt without upsetting the French people, who frankly have got used to a superb service and have sometimes abused it. The government have introduced the idea that you should go to your GP before you make an appointment with a specialist. This is to try to discourage people who go from one specialist to another because they don't like the diagnosis or treatment prescribed by the first. They are trying to be a bit more sensible than before when women went off to a health farm or spa in order to lose weight (paid at 70% by the state). They are trying to get people to accept generic drugs on their prescriptions rather than the big brands to save money. And yet, so deep is the idea of customer choice, that none of these measures is obligatory. I have heard people in the *pharmacie* refusing to accept generic drugs saying they are used to the brand they've always had. You can still go to various specialists if you want; you just get less back from the state for the appointment fee.

'Okay, okay!' you are saying, but the NHS in the UK is free at the point of service and you have to pay in France. This is true. Up to a point. The French system pays between 60% and 70% of everything to do with health including dental treatment and opticians' bills. This means when I go to see my GP (no appointment necessary), I personally have to pay €7 and the two items on my prescription cost me personally

€9 a month. How much do you pay for your prescription if you are under retirement age?

For all life-threatening diseases, listed by the state you get 100% paid, including hospitalisation, treatments and doctors' fees. These diseases include anything to do with the heart (as in Eric's case – he had the triple by-pass here in France 17 years ago, totally free, including five weeks in a convalescent home for about €5 a day), diabetes, cancer, mental illnesses and a list of others. That leaves a lot of non-life threatening illnesses and over 90 % of French residents pay for private top-up insurance to cover them for all these cases.

We haven't taken out extra insurance – mainly because at our ages (61 and 71), the monthly premiums would be around €150 a month and we think that's too much. Some of our friends think we are irresponsible in not taking out this extra insurance but let me tell you what our experience has been over seven years, bearing in mind an insurance saving of (€150 x 12 x 7 =) €12,600.

We have had four brushes with illness apart from Eric's recent heart incident. Several years ago Eric had an operation to remove a cataract. The specialist said that would be covered at 100%, with just €15 (30% of a consultation fee) to pay. I had a minor operation on my wrist to open up the carpel tunnel. The specialist told me he usually does more serious stuff so it wasn't worth charging for. That operation cost me another €15.

Three years ago, Eric had a second hip replacement (the first one which was performed in England had dislodged – apparently not enough cement was put in it) This time the consultant was the top man at the university hospital and he decided my husband would be a private patient, so we were holding our breath for his bill. It came to about £400 which was a proportion of his fees not paid for by the state. Everything else was paid for except a 'solidarity' fee of €15 a day to the hospital - just an aside here to mention that a friend of ours in Lancashire had her hip replaced privately and paid £8,000.

And the latest instance is this back operation for me. I suppose it is embarrassing having to ask how much it will cost rather than know the insurance company will pick up the bill, but it does re-enforce the idea that you are a customer as well as a patient. It is going to cost me €300 (proportion of the consultant's fees and the daily solidarity charge of €16 per day for five days in hospital).

You would think that having to pay something, however little, stops us going to the doctor for nothing and yet, maybe the opposite is true because most people in France have the extra insurance, and they want value for their money. The French swallow the biggest quantity of tablets in the western world – you should see the carrier bags full coming out of the chemist's. They even have a word for the stress of running a home and being a mother (*surmenage*) for which you can have a doctor's note and be sent on a *cure*.

I am not sure if they are hypochondriacs or just have a high expectation of well-being. The *pharmacies* have a monopoly on tablets – you can't even buy an aspirin anywhere else, and the *pharmacie* is the poshest shop in any village however poor the rest of it is.

The French being made responsible for their own records and results has another effect I believe: they are more knowledgeable about the body than most of us Brits. They don't have just a sore throat here – they have pharyngitis, laryngitis or *une angine* (swollen glands). My friend showed me a rash on her arm and said 'Look at this urticaria'. Urticaria? To us a lot of spots are a rash. They know the technical term for everything. To me, my stomach is anything between my rib-cage and my bottom, a French person will specify, abdomen, intestines, etc. We have a collar-bone, they have a *clavicule*. I certainly didn't know where my liver was until I came to live here. That is their biggest health hang-up - *une crise de foie*. I must say the symptoms sound much like a hang-over to me. Well, it's either a liver crisis or women complain about heavy legs, *jambes lourdes*. Every time I go into the *pharmacie* I see cures for heavy legs – I wish I knew what they were.

Back in the neurologist's surgery, with a model of a spine on his desk to help me understand my problem, Dr Adam explained that the fusion operation is a simple one taking about one hour and that after a few days I should be ready to go home. After a couple of weeks at home, however, he said he wants me to go to the Spa hotel at Granville by the sea of re-education, physiotherapy and exercise for three weeks.

I blanched as the good doctor was telling me this, thinking *he* was thinking I am better off than I am. So I asked him the embarrassing question. 'Madame Barker,' he said, 'If I prescribe this treatment it will cost you nothing but the daily solidarity charge.' So in October I'm off to the health spa at the seaside. I must remember not to go on about our biggest English hang-up: constipation. The French don't know what it is.

19 Driving You Mad
December 1999 / January 2010

Once off the ferry or out of the tunnel you can breathe more easily and relax as you drive on endless kilometres of quiet roads to your destination. Okay, so you have to pay tolls if you use the motorways but there is no car tax to pay if you are resident here, and after all, taking the motorway is a choice and not an obligation.

You must be safer because French drivers are better-trained too, because you can't just have your dad or your mum teach you. You have to have a proper driving course with a driving school and even when you pass – at age eighteen, not seventeen, you have to drive around for a year with a big red 'A' stuck in your back window to let other road-users know you are a newbie.

Just to be even safer, on motorways and main roads the speed limit is lowered in wet weather to 110kmh on motorways and 80kmh on main roads (*routes nationales*).

What is more, the police are much more in evidence here as are the ubiquitous speed cameras which can lead to points deducted from your working total of 12 if you exceed the limit. You can have your driving licence taken from you on the spot if you are caught travelling at more than 25kmh above the limit.

As a visitor to France, you needn't worry too much about speed cameras and parking tickets. Sure, your number will be taken down but just as in the UK at the moment, foreign number plates are a no-go area for the authorities as it is just too hard to chase them up. They are working on a European-wide system, but it may be some time yet. As a European commission spokesman has said, 'The record and the fine just go straight in the bin.'

Another safety feature are the small, extra lights low down at traffic lights which can be clearly viewed by the car nearest to them and this means motorists have no need to guess when they are going to change. For good measure, they change straight from red to green; the amber is by-passed so that drivers are discouraged from revving up and setting off on the amber.

The police (or *gendarmes* outside larger towns) also have the right to give you an on-the-spot fine and can randomly check for drink-driving without any excuse. We were once in a long queue at a traffic light where the police were gathered and the whole line of cars was breathalysed. Believe it or not, the alcohol driving limit is stricter in France at 0.5 milligrams per millilitre of blood rather than 0.8 in the UK.

Finally, you are obliged to carry your driving licence, insurance documents and your *carte grise* (logbook) with you when driving. You don't want to give the *gendarmes* any excuse to fine you.

French people on the whole, keep their cars longer than British people do. That's why second-hand cars keep a higher value over here. You see many more cars for sale privately (notices stuck in rear car-windows). When I asked my students how people could feel protected without any guarantee, they reminded me that, as in the case of selling property, and the buyer can prove that the seller knew of a fault, the law will make the seller pay compensation. This is the law of *vices cachés*.

In England you know how old a car is from the registration number. In France it's much harder to date as you have to change your registration when you move from one department (county) to another. In France, you can't be sure how old a car is, but you know where it is from – the last two digits are the post code for the department. For example, around here it is 14 for the Calvados, so we can identify Parisians and visitors from other regions, not just foreigners.

Now, I have an old, ten year old Peugeot and in reverse snobbery mode, boasted of it to a group of students who work in Research and Development, all university-qualified engineers, mature and earning well. I was really put out when they boasted of the ages of their cars – in fact the winner was the proud owner of a 16 year-old Renault Espace. Of course it was bound to be a Renault, a Citroen or a Peugeot since 70% of French people are patriotic enough to stick to French makes. I wonder what state English car manufacturing would be in now, if English people had taken the same patriotic decision.

So they buy French but keep their car as long as it will last out instead of 'keeping up with the Jones' by buying a new one every two years. I suppose it's only one step beyond this non-materialistic view of cars, not to bother much about cleaning them. None of those students regularly cleaned their car – twice a year was the norm. In England, on a Sunday morning in suburbia, you'll see, not a line of people returning from church, but a line of buckets and hoses as men religiously wash and polish their cars on the drive. What else is a drive for?

So, given the *gendarmerie's* penchant for random stops, the exact speed limits, the strict alcohol limits and the professional driving lesson all French drivers have had, you can relax and enjoy your driving experience in France. Or perhaps not.

Take one single fact. Despite having miles more road for roughly the same number of people, road deaths are much higher in France. Craig McGinty writes in 'Travel' magazine, *'There are 8000 road deaths a year in France compared to 3,500 in Britain... France, with over 20 deaths every day has the worst road safety record of any large industrial nation... If you add the 30,000 plus people who are crippled or seriously injured annually, French roads are a permanent tragedy.'*

It is true. Not only do you frequently drive past floral tributes and plaques where people have been killed, in some parts of France there are grisly black above-life size silhouettes representing, one or two people, or a whole family who were slaughtered at that spot. There are shock TV advertising campaigns meant to shame motorists into driving more reasonably, but once behind a wheel French drivers (and particularly men I'm afraid) cannot bear to be behind another vehicle and will overtake in the most hair-raising situations. Well, it may be a way of letting off steam after being so polite all day at work in shops and at restaurants. Or maybe it's simply because they can.

Despite over six million random breath tests per year, only one in a hundred is found to be over the limit. Everyone knows this is rubbish. Even the lorry drivers, who depend on driving for a living, routinely drink wine and cider at the *Relais Routiers* (literally transport cafés but a lot better quality food and great value). Not so long ago, regulars would have their bottle re-corked and kept for the next visit. I'm not saying they all drink over the limit, but drinking alcohol with meals is the norm – indeed when most country people talk about *alcool* they mean strong spirits, not wine.

There is a theory that the police and the government are scared of people power. The same power that enables farmers to close supermarkets by dumping manure at their doors or that allows lorry drivers to close down the Channel Tunnel, or fishermen to block the channel ports. Minor infractions are part of the game to French drivers – it's us against the authorities. An oncoming driver will flash his lights to warn you of police presence ahead. Always driving a bit over the speed limit is okay too. Some of my students have boasted of never buying a parking ticket and never having had a fine - another finger up at authority.

Of course speed cameras don't run scared of drivers, but I personally know at least two people who, when almost at the points limit, merely claimed their spouse or even their mother was driving, in order to save their licence.

Even when your licence is taken away and you are theoretically banned from driving, you can drive a *micro car*. There is quite a big market for these tiny cars, limited in weight up to 350kg unloaded and they can apparently go up to 90kmh. Now that they can boast of being environmentally friendly too, any slight stigma of driving a 'toy' car is fast waning. These cars have become particularly popular in the big towns where parking is difficult. These micro-cars can be parked at right-angles so you can drive straight at the kerb and stop. You can even get out and lift your car to juggle it into position. Mind you, even in a normal car, People leave their hand-brakes off in Paris as it is very likely somebody will drive in to park in front of you and shunt your car backwards to make room.

For us in the country, the most dangerous roads are the country lanes. They are so quiet that drivers are lulled into a false sense of security and fail to slow down at bends and they overtake on blind brows. Because the tarmac is limited you are often forced into the dirt on the side by inconsiderate drivers.

Beware in particular the young driver – the one with an 'A' notice in the rear window. He has passed his test within the last year and testosterone is raging. Accidents involving motorbikes, like in the U.K., are even more frequent. We all know motorbikes are dangerous, but here, death on a motorbike seems to be raised to hero status when you see the engraved monuments in the cemeteries. Over 20% of road casualties are bikers. Add to this the youngsters aged 14 or over who can ride a moped up to 50cc and you can see how a motorcyclist is 14 times more likely to have an accident as a car driver.

For me, the scariest driving custom is a left-over from Napoleonic times and is the right of drivers to pull out of a road on the right, even if that road is a minor one. True, most of these *priorités à droite* have been suppressed but sometimes, and without any road sign, a vehicle will pull out. I don't know how many accidents are directly caused by this rule but just occasionally, a French driver takes it into his head to apply this rule at a roundabout and just heads on out thinking he has priority over the vehicles already on it.

When all is said and done, with less opportunity for speeding on the roads in most parts of the UK because there are so many vehicles, you are definitely safer in the UK than in France.

No licence needed for Micro cars

Parking at right angles in Paris

20 Ce N'est Pas Le Cricket
February / March 2010

It is interesting to realise there really is a difference in attitudes to sporting etiquette on either side of the channel. Let me cite a few examples.

You may have heard about it at the time. I mean of course the France versus Ireland football match to qualify for the World Cup in 2010. The French won but spectators had witnessed the captain, Thierry Henry, handling the ball, although the ref apparently didn't. After the match, Henry was seen commiserating with the Irish with a hang-dog expression on his face. So, the next day, after the cameras showed that he had undoubtedly handled the ball (twice), gaining a crucial goal for his team, the Irish and all of Britain was up in arms. Henry had to admit it. Or rather, he admitted the ball had hit his hand. However, he maintained it was up to the ref to spot it and it wasn't his fault if the ref hadn't. Remember, Thierry Henry was the captain of the French team. Not much of a role-model for his team and younger players. The media went crazy. 'Hand of Frog!' was my favourite headline (a play on words of Maradonna's 'hand of God' in 1986).

An even more blatant incident occurred in the 2006 World Cup Final when Zinadine Zidane head-butted an Italian player (the ref didn't see that either). France lost that one, but Zidane was treated as a hero by the French – in contrast to David Beckham in his early days when, lying on the ground in another World Cup match, he kicked a player standing at his side. Beckham was sent off and vilified by the English press and fans – the English don't hero-worship players who don't play fair.

Then there was Eric Cantona, who after a spectator shouted at him from the crowd, leapt over the barrier and took a flying kick at the man who had shouted insulting language at him. Whilst the fans bayed for his blood in the first instance, the British public sided with him when they heard the fan had insulted Cantona's mother. Last year, Cantona's film 'Looking For Eric' hit the cinemas and the man in the crowd, Matthew Simmons, more than 14 years later, whined, 'I get phone calls taunting me and threatening me.'

The Thierry Henry incident has had an unexpected twist. It appears he has not been lionised for his cheating, after all. In fact, the French Newspaper *Le Monde* had a poll just the following week asking who deserved to go to the World Cup – France or Ireland. Over 80,000 French people responded to the poll with more than 80% saying that Ireland deserved to go through. The French said they were actually embarrassed by their undeserved success.

It goes to show you can't be too sweeping about national characteristics. There are always exceptions to the rule.

A golfing friend of my husband's went to his local café, '*La Civette*' in Falaise, Normandy, the day after the match. An old regular, who winds his scarf around his Labrador's neck to catch the old dog's dribble, turned round mournfully on his bar stool and hung his head saying, 'Sorry, Tony. Thierry Henry should know that he has hands and he has feet and the two of them should not be confused.' Can't resist philosophising, the French, can they? That was nearly as good as Cantona's 'seagulls and sardines' one.

So, is there a difference in attitudes to sporting etiquette? Certainly, Patrice Evra, who plays fullback for Manchester United thinks so. He has said he has been very disappointed by the behaviour of French fans. 'I don't understand,' he said. 'The fans should be behind us. When you play at the Stade de France, you often hear boos after only five minutes.' He contrasted this behaviour with that at Old Trafford. 'When we lost, there was applause, not boos,' he said. 'It's a matter of culture.'

It all comes back to the idea of fair play. The French call it *le fair play* because they haven't a word for it. In general, if there isn't a word for something in a particular language, the notion doesn't exist. For example, we have no English word for the German *'schadenfraude'*- taking pleasure in other people's misfortunes, presumably because we don't, or don't admit to doing so.

Is it only the English who really understand the notion of fair play? The 1950s duo, Flanders and Swan sang in their gentle lampooning of The English, that anyone who is not English, just cannot understand what 'playing up and playing the game' is all about.

> *And all the world over each nation's the same*
> *They've simply no notion of playing the game;*
> *They argue with umpires, they cheer when they've won,*
> *And they practise beforehand which ruins the fun!*

Not two weeks after the Thierry Henry incident, Arsenal played Manchester City and were beaten 3-0. At the end of the match, the Arsenal manager, Frenchman Arsene Wenger refused to shake hands with his counterpart, Mark Hughes.

Mark Hughes commented, 'I have been to the Emirate Stadium and been beaten 6-2 but I still offer my hand. It's the best you can do. There are certain protocols and maybe on this occasion Arsene has not worked with that.' There you are. Whether you call it protocol, etiquette, fair-play, or playing the game, it was not observed by Monsieur Wenger, whose argument when pressed was, 'Well, I think that has not a lot to do with the game. I'm free to shake hands with whom I want after the game. I have nothing more to say about that.' Asked if it was not professional courtesy to shake an opposing manager's hand, Wenger added, 'Yes it is. I had no professional courtesy.' Wow! So he does understand the etiquette, but disagrees with it? Or he doesn't care about 'playing the game'?

Certainly English men who play golf with Frenchmen report covertly that the French don't stick to the spirit of the rules. They think nothing of nudging a ball, or quite obviously throwing it out of the undergrowth, or declaring their own 'Mulligan' when really, the British way is to offer a Mulligan (a second shot from the tee without penalty) to one's opponents.

Maybe it's not that the French are cheaters; but that they just don't see why such niceties have anything to do with sport – after all, from their point of view, you are there to win whatever you are playing, otherwise there is no point playing at all. Maybe they just can't be bothered with the trivialness of fair play. Is that perhaps why the French don't play cricket? Heck, they don't even play French cricket. And why should they? Most of us Brits don't understand the rules of cricket – you know the ones:

You have two sides – one out in the field and one in.
Each man that's in the side that's in goes out and when he's out he comes in and the next man goes in until he's out.
When they are all out the side that's out comes in and the side that's been in goes out and tries to get those coming in out.
Sometimes you get men still in and not out.
When both sides have been in and out including the not outs, that's the end of the game.

It's quite reasonable that the French can't see the point of a game where you can play for five days and still end up with a draw. Actually, I have read that some brave French men and a lot of ex-pat Brits are trying to introduce the game in France. The rules are so complicated they have resorted to a cartoon to try to simplify it all. For example, there is an illustration to show the various ways a batsman can be 'out'. I have found ten such cartoons trying to explain the rules of the game.

Why faff about for five days for no result playing cricket, when you can sally forth from your garden from September throughout the winter shooting pheasant, deer, partridge, wild boar, pigeons and rabbits and then take them home to prepare for dinner? Hunting, in France, is only second to football as a pastime.

Hunting and shooting has been the right of every Frenchman since the Revolution gave all the lands of the aristocracy to the people. A quarter of the land surface area of France is *Forêt domaniale* - meaning land belonging to the state. Only the state in this case is the *République* or people of France. So you don't have to pay to shoot in these woods – it's your right as a Frenchman. I don't suppose there is much scope for *le fair play* in shooting, it's just you against the unarmed opponent which you will later eat.

An English friend of ours runs a fishing lake and is quietly offended by the French fishermen who come and catch fish and actually take them home to eat them- even the carp. English fishermen are much more likely to catch them and throw them back. Is this fair play gone mad? I must say I'm on the side of the French here as I can see no point in ripping a fish's lip for no reason except to say that you caught it in fair play.

Could it be possible that our idea of fair play is too effete, too limp-wristed for the French? That offering a contentious point to the opponent, cheering for the underdog and throwing back your catch is a bridge too far? If that is the case, then cricket has no chance of becoming popular over here.

21. Women's Stuff
April / May 2010

We were doing one of our favourite things in Lisieux; people-watching whilst sitting in a café. Well, not exactly *in* a café, as the café has a tarpaulin extension where everybody gathers. You can understand why the smokers ensconce themselves there – even to eat lunch in January – it's the last stand of the smoker, banned from inside public places. Companies making these temporary extensions complete with plastic windows, must be making a bomb. The smokers are more tenacious here in France. You see groups gathered around the entrance to any office, round the back of the supermarkets and rather alarmingly, if you take the stairs in the hospital in Caen instead of the lift, you see the stairs bestrewn with *magots* (fag-ends), where the staff congregate on their breaks.

I'm not a smoker (not since 8 years ago anyway) but I want to be out there too. I don't want to miss out on the people-watching. Le Gentleman Café in Lisieux is definitely the place to be for people-watching as it's on the corner of the market and the main shopping street and just about everybody passes by if you sit long enough, which over here you can do, of course. The waiter would never ask if you've finished and hint that the table is needed. The service is quick and cheerful and the prices are okay for France (you pay over £2 for a tea or a simple coffee anywhere). The toilet is pretty bad though – only one cubicle and to get there you have to pass behind any gentleman standing at the *pissoir*.

So on a Saturday morning, after parking the car well out of town to give us some exercise, and after doing the rounds of the market and looking to see if the sales are on in the clothes shops, we end up just before lunchtime at Le Gentleman.

On this particular morning, as on others, we were looking surreptitiously at the passers-by to see if we could identify any English people. We both reckon we can spot an English person, even before he or she speaks. That morning we tried to list the physical traits English people have. We could come up with only a possible two: that English people have rosier skin, and that there are more English people with curly hair.

We see now that 'the English rose' is a true description of a pretty, rosy-cheeked Englishwoman, who blushes easily. French people tend to have mat or olive complexions and don't blush as easily. Also there are fewer French people with red or curly hair. In George Sempé's ever-popular 'Le Petit Nicholas' stories, when an English boy arrives in school, he is called George and has sandy-coloured curly hair and buck teeth. That is the French idea of a typical English schoolboy.

Now, I'm going to stick my neck out and say English women are prettier than French women. I'm allowed. I've been travelling, studying, 'twinning', working and living in France for over 30 years. Believe me, English women are indeed more naturally beautiful even though I realise beauty is in the eye of the beholder. Their faces are definitely more symmetrical, their colouring healthier and skin much more flawless. However, I have to admit that French women are more attractive. By 'attractive' I mean, after taking into account the whole package. The way they dress, walk, do their hair and hold themselves; French women win hands down. They know how to present themselves – a nonchalantly knotted scarf here, a matching handbag there, a smart hairdo always. There is a French expression *jolie-laide* (pretty and ugly at the same time, not 'quite ugly') which doesn't exist in English. For the English, you are either beautiful or not, but for the French, a woman can be quite plain and yet sexually attractive.

I have concluded that it's all in the presentation. Certainly the presence of a *coiffeur* in every village, along with the *pharmacie* and the *boulangerie* tells us a lot. I don't know any Frenchwoman, for example, who colours her own hair as I did for years in England. Going to the hairdresser is as essential as buying a daily baguette, and this despite 80% of French workers being paid the minimum wage.

Last month's Northern Life magazine had some nostalgic photos of the North-West in the early sixties and one photo caught my imagination. It was of two teenage girls out in town wearing headscarves over hair-rollers. I remember having done that myself and looking at the picture again I couldn't for the life of me understand why we did that. You can bet your life Frenchwomen didn't do that in the sixties, and wouldn't do it nowadays. They are not seen out without looking their best - hair and all. I hear that in England, young mothers sometimes wear their pyjamas under their coat to take their children to school. I was asking a visiting friend from England last week if this was true and she said not only was it true, but that Tesco have decided to ban women shopping in their pyjamas. This would be unthinkable here. Maybe it's the result of 24 hour shopping in England, which is much rarer over here – in fact, Sunday shopping in general is much rarer over here.

I have mentioned before the fact that the average Frenchwoman is slimmer than her English counterpart – she just eats less and smokes more. She spends time on herself and makes more effort. She matches her outfits and accessorises them and isn't afraid of standing out in a crowd. In fact, this is exactly what she *wants* to do.

This afternoon I went shopping for a dress for a very special holiday. I found a nice shop with suitable dresses. The saleswoman was pencil thin, much tanned (and when I asked where she had been at this time of year, she told me she cheats and goes to a sunbed place) and immaculately made-up. I was white, flabby and dithering. I tried four dresses on and she sweetly told me to avoid two which showed my plump upper-arms and to avoid a colour which made me look pale. She wouldn't let me buy just anything. This woman wasn't beautiful or even pretty but boy, did she look good and I bet she felt good too.

So, apart from the effort, there must be the question of knowhow. Why is it that a fine scarf tied around my neck is likely to look more like a bandage than a glamour accessory? Why is it I would never go to an office job wearing jeans with floaty tops and lots of bangles? Because I'm English of course.

The difference starts at a young age. A French mother will buy her daughter's first make-up and show her how to put it on, how to knot that scarf around her neck and which earrings go well with her outfit (not mind you, when the daughter is ten, but more likely when she is eighteen).

In England, when I was young, parents looked at their daughters as they were trying to get out of the front door to go to the Mecca and would say something like, 'You're not going out looking like that. Get that muck off your face.' Even now, my husband will tell me how he likes me to look 'natural' by which he means he means he doesn't like me wearing much make-up, but I guarantee that if we go to a party, he can be found keenly talking to the most made-up woman in the room. Why? Because he's English. His wife and daughter are not to be only modestly attractive.

We English do not build up the confidence of our young. Somehow we feel it is boastful of us to tell them how beautiful or clever they are. Kate Fox, in her excellent book 'Watching the English' tells how we find it difficult to accept compliments and how we lack confidence. The French have a saying, *'Etre bien dans sa peau'* (to feel good in one's skin). And they do.

I remember, being struck by a group of my French students in their forties, learning adjectives in English. They all sat round in a circle showing photos and describing the people in them. I was smiling wryly to myself as they happily described their husbands as 'handsome', their sons as 'very intelligent' their girls as 'beautiful' and had no coyness or embarrassment about saying so. I am sure a similar group of English people would be busy playing down the attributes of their loved ones so as not to seem smug and vain.

I have just been discussing this article with a friend who travels between England and France for her work. Two weeks ago she was in Harrogate at the French Property Show. One of her colleagues, a young French woman called

Veronique, turned up late and was distraught at not having had the time for a manicure and hairdo before arriving at the show. It really knocked her confidence, but three days later, my friend saw her again and asked her how things had gone. Veronique said she would be glad to get back to her beautician but she had felt all right at the show, 'because English women don't bother, do they?'

French women will pay more for their clothes but own fewer. They would be amazed if they could see the amount of clothes a lot of my English friends own. It is not unusual for an Englishwoman's clothes to fill the wardrobes in two bedrooms. French women's clothes hardly fill one wardrobe. They buy better quality and fewer clothes. They know exactly what they have and what accessories they need to go with them. In every small town you see a shop for *Retouches* (alterations). I think I am right in saying you would have trouble finding somebody to do this in England. In France they are smart shops. So Frenchwomen keep their clothes longer and have them remodelled. They don't throw them out whilst they are still in good condition either. There is the Red Cross who will take your old clothes and an odd 'designer' second-hand clothes shop in big towns, but nothing like the phenomenon of charity clothes shops that exist in England. When I asked around my French friends if they rummage around in charity shops, they didn't know what I was talking about. So Frenchwomen buy fewer, but better quality clothes and keep them longer.

Such a shame. We really could learn from French women. If English women could add the *savoir-faire* of the French to their natural beauty, there wouldn't be any women more attractive than the English anywhere.

The River Dives
August / September 2010

The longer we live here, the closer we realise are the ties between this part of Normandy and England. You cannot do better than travel the 105 kilometres along the river Dives from the English Channel to its source in the Orne department to trace the multiple connections between the two countries.

At Dives-sur-Mer, William the Conqueror amassed his ships in preparation for the invasion of England. In the town's old church of Notre Dame, you can see an engraved list of those of William's compatriots who sailed to England with him. They are in alphabetical order of first names, showing how surnames were little used at the time.

As the Dives winds inland and crosses Le Marais, the once treacherous area of marshes which the Germans flooded and where many a parachutist drowned in WW2, you pass the sites of no less than five bridges which, along with the famous Pegasus Bridge, were destroyed on the 6th June 1944 in order to prevent the Germans sending reinforcements to the landing beaches.

During the centuries that followed the Norman conquest of England, many English soldiers launched a succession of invasions attempting to secure English kings' rights to land in Normandy / Maine and farther south, Aquitaine and Gascony. On occasions there were even attempts to realise the English kings' dreams of securing the French throne based on often quite legitimate claims. During the time of

Joan of Arc, for instance, in the first decades of the 15th century, the English were an occupying force, often raiding Norman towns and villages and regarded as hostile by the local inhabitants. It is, however, very likely that some of the English invaders would have settled in some villages and localities and eventually integrated into Norman society.

The word 'English' is reflected in the place and church names along the river such as Englesqueville and St Marie aux Anglais (note the preposition *'aux'* changes the meaning slightly – 'Saint Mary belonging to the English'). These places remind us that from the time that William the Conqueror was both king of England and Duke of Normandy, until the end of the Hundred Years War in 1453, there were a large number of English people living in Normandy, just as there were French living in England.

Certainly I am surprised to find these traces of English in Normandy so long ago. And yet, it makes sense since William took his henchmen to live in England. Wouldn't they go back periodically and take their wives and families? When they went back after a generation or two, wouldn't they be designated 'English' by the locals?

Farther into the hinterland is a village called Beaumais, it is small and pretty with a church and an ancient *manoir* – like any other village in these parts, and through which I have frequently driven.

Now, like a lot of other people, I have on and off, tried to trace my family roots. In particular, my maiden name Stubbs, simply because it's a bit out of the ordinary in Lancashire and sticking to one name is easier than going back up the maternal line. I knew already that it's an old name, and that there were a lot of Stubbs in Staffordshire, but I recently discovered that Stubbs were Norwegian, that is, Norsemen or Normans, and they came over to England during the time of William the Conqueror and were given lands in Bloxwich and Water- Eaton in Staffordshire. As if this were not exciting enough, I then saw a reference to *'elaborate accounts of this family's descent from Belmeis or Beaumais in Calvados in Normandy through Richard Belmeis, the founder of the family who was a follower of Roger de Montgomery who was the first Earl of Shrewsbury and later Bishop of London about 1100'.*

What is sure is that 'Stubbs' is not a French word, although it could be Norman, but as I discovered in the church in Dives-sur-Mer, surnames were not in common usage around then. So maybe there is some connection between my family from a thousand years ago, and a village on the Dives very near where I now live. So I may have come back to my roots.

Even further and almost at its source, the Dives runs through Chambois, another battle site of WW2, where in the middle of August 1944, a large pincer movement involving American forces moving up from the south east and British and Canadian forces moving in from the north-west (Trun), managed to encircle thousands of German forces in what has become known as the Falaise Pocket. The only escape for enemy troops was at Montormel near Chambois and this escape route was blocked by a very brave force of Polish troops. In all, the Poles lost 2300 men but in a stunning display of valour, they sealed the fate of the German forces in Normandy, and Paris was taken only a few days later.

There have been connections over a thousand years between the River Dives and the English, so it should come as no surprise that a form of Anglo-Normand was spoken around here for a couple of centuries before the French language took over.

And, during all that time, downstream from Chambois, St. Pierre-sur–Dives has straddled the river, dominating all it surveyed from its important abbey with a solar calendar marked out on the floor of the nave. There is a small hole in the roof which catches the sun's rays at 12 noon and the light strikes the calendar to indicate the month.

Because it was the last fordable town on the river before the sea, and because there was a need for trading between the cereal growing farmers of the flat plains around Falaise and Caen, and the dairy farmers in the undulating Pays d'Auge, a market grew up in St Pierre-sur-Dives which has been in situ for more than a thousand years. The land belonged to the monks at the abbey and so it was in their interest to support the market and they built a magnificent market hall of impressive proportions.

I wish I could say that the present market hall is the original, but that was burnt down during WW2. The present structure was painstakingly reproduced soon after the war and the market continues as it always has.

You would have some difficulty explaining what a 'farmers' market' is to the locals. A French market is always a farmers' market – what else could it be? Only because English markets deteriorated into collections of cheaply-produced clothes and goods (most likely from Taiwan), did they have to re-invent the idea of local markets.

Here in St. Pierre you see local produce in abundance; from a stall which might sell nothing but different varieties of potatoes or olives, right to the other extreme of a little old lady farmer at a table selling a plucked chicken or a couple of quails, along with some herbs and some fresh, untreated cream, say. You do wonder what the British health and safety people would have to say if you tried selling your home-produced food in this honest but amateurish way. There is even a stall where a lady sells nothing but different sorts of mushroom. And the fish? I have never understood why, in an island nation like ours, there is not much more choice and accessibility to fish, and why we are not at all as adventurous in our fish tastes as are the French. As a fish-market man at Trouville said to me, after telling me he had worked on the markets in the south of England for a while, 'I know you English. For you, fish is trout, salmon or cod. You know nothing else.' I couldn't argue with him. I have yet to try whelks, *lotte*, bass or the many other fish on offer here. In St Pierre-sur-Dives there is an entire walkway lined with fish stalls. Typical local foodstuffs in these parts are home-made cider and *pommeau* (a fortified cider); soft cheeses like *Camembert, Pont L'Eveque* and goat's cheese; *teurgoule* (a spicy rice pudding with cinnamon served cold) and wonderful hams which you can buy whole or have slices carved off. Just now in June, the strawberries from Falaise are small and bursting with flavour. You just sit back and watch your guests dip them in water and eat them without any accompaniment for a perfect natural taste.

Animals for keeping and eating are sold alive too - all manner of chicken and ducks are popular, along with rabbits (for eating, not for keeping). The last time we were there, there were two boys selling their rabbits on the steps on the market hall. Tradition starts at a young age around here.

The link with the past is not broken yet. The knife-grinder still wanders around the market for people to stop him whilst he sharpens their scissors and knives. This reminds me of the rag and bone man who came round the streets of our northern towns until the sixties, giving the housewives cakes of 'donkey-stone' with which to whiten the doorstep, in exchange for old clothes.

The children's ride is no gimmicky machine with music, it's the real thing with ponies tied to a central post, walking round and round.

The market has hardly changed over the centuries. You can imagine too, some of this produce being rowed down the river to the sea at Dives-sur-Mer and across to markets in England - yet another link between our two countries.

23 Farmer's Delight
October / November 2010

Time and time again we meet people who come out to live in France only to go 'back home' after a few years (some people have worked out the average stay is two years for those who go back). The reasons given are: a failure to learn the language enough to be able to mix socially, a lack of money due to a business idea failing, a mistaken idea of thinking you can live on practically nothing, and missing newly-born grandchildren or having unhappy teenagers who can't settle in France.

I went to talk to a couple who bucked the trend big-style by moving here 27 years ago and who have no intention of going back. They are Tim and Chrissie Green who hail from Nantwich, Cheshire, and who had three daughters, Cherry, Abigail and Beth, who were 7, 5 and 3 respectively when they landed in Normandy in 1983. Tim had trained at agricultural college in Shropshire and worked as manager for a farm in Scotland which was run by *The Farmers' Weekly* magazine. The magazine had wanted for some time to send a farmer to run a farm in France, from where he would report on conditions and life in general for perusal by their readers. It took the magazine ten years to comply with the French bureaucracy in order to get hold of their farm in Normandy.

The farm is the home farm of a chateau which is still owned by a member of the aristocracy, although the farm is now an independent business. In those days, the move was quite pioneering and Chrissie remembers contacting the British embassy in Paris to ask if the domestic appliances would work in France and being told that they didn't know. At the last minute too, they received a communication to say that they needed papers prepared by the veterinary service so that they could export their sheepdog. It was their last day and as they set off on their journey to the ferry, the vet rush up and thrust the correct documents through the car window.

The farmhouse is just as you dream a farmhouse should be. The living rooms are on the first floor as the basement houses workrooms, so the windows in the kitchen and living-room look out away over the fields and hills. The kitchen is enormous with a table to match. Just about everything happens here; cooking, sewing, planning, discussing, family meals (often with farmworkers and young people on work experience on the farm) and my interview. The other living room is another huge square room with a magnificent open fireplace where the dogs lie curled on a winter's evening.

Neither Tim nor Chrissie spoke much French at all when they arrived and it was Tim who was thrown in the deep end as he retained the existing French foreman and another farm-worker. However, as Tim pointed out, when you hear the same words repeated all day, every day, and all about the farm, you learn quickly. Now, farming isn't my area of expertise, so when Tim tested my French on the spot - did I know the French for 'udder'? I hadn't a clue. Chrissie admits she took longer to gain fluency as her duties lay with the three girls and so her opportunities for learning French were limited to the school gate.

The reason for being asked to run the farm by *The Farmers' Weekly* was to compare dairy-farming in the UK and France. Tim wrote a column over twenty-odd years for the magazine and was also invited to speak in the UK and in Paris at agricultural gatherings. Soon groups of farmers and interested parties wanted to come to see the farm in Normandy and Chrissie had to cultivate her skills of catering for groups of up to 50 people at a time – two or three times a week providing picnic lunches in the old cider press. Besides this, Chrissie started her own column reporting on her life as a farmer's wife in Normandy.

Farming in France nowadays is just as hard as in England, Tim says. In the early days, he could see certain advantages for French farmers, but not now. It's a hard grind wherever you are. If Tim leaves the cowman to do the milking in order to take a Sunday off, he still has to do all the other jobs when he gets back.

The farm produces milk from a dairy herd, which goes into the local cheeses: *Livarot*, *Camembert* and *Pont L'Evêque* – cheeses which have a long tradition and which are taken very seriously by the producers and consumers alike. Soon, Tim was invited to join the *Confrérie* (the guild of Livarot cheese-makers and further improved his language skills at the dinners, speeches and meetings these organisations are fond of. It was a short step to be invited to be a councillor for the commune, or parish. Over the years, it has been Tim's English which has proved a boon, for nowadays 10% of their commune are English people and when they have a dilemma, Tim is roped in to sort it out.

Tim remembers one English couple who were renting out their *gîte* for the first time and noticed the water in the swimming-pool was green. They hastily emptied the pool and started to fill it from the kitchen tap. Soon they realised it was going to take days and the guests were due the next day. So they rang the mayor who informed them they would need the permission of the *SAUR* (the water board) as the consumption of water for a pool is outside the normal domestic volume. They were dismayed since the guests would expect a pool the next day. Over to Tim, who thought he would help out by filling his 5 cubic metre tank from their own spring water (thus not using the water board's water). He towed the tanker by tractor to the *gîte* where a line of children and adults were waiting around the pool for their first swim. They were devastated to see the tank fill no more than two inches. Altogether, Tim spent his whole weekend, and fifteen trips with his tanker. Such are the calls upon friendly councillor-farmers.

Chrissie and Tim have nothing but praise for the education system in France, especially the fact that the girls went through various schools: local up to 11, nearby by bus up to 15, in a further big town up to 18 where they boarded Monday to Friday (funded by the state), and then to university in Caen, where they started to stay over some weekends for social reasons. The eldest daughter, Cherry, finally went after Caen to the famous Sorbonne in Paris and got the *Aggregation*, the highest competitive teaching qualification in France.

Beth, the youngest daughter, wanted to have a year in an English school, so went to stay with relatives in Cheshire, to do the fourth year at secondary level. Although it was an interesting experience for her, she did notice how precocious the English girls were in their behaviour with the boys and that the curriculum was somewhat behind the

French one, so that she had a lot of work to catch up when she got back to France.

Cherry and Beth are both teachers of English in secondary schools and Abigail is a professional actor who is now playing Ophelia in Hamlet, in Caen. Although Chrissie feels they would all have done well in England also, being bi-lingual in France has given them an edge in their careers. All three have French partners and now there are three grandchildren too. In fact, two weddings have been held at the farm in the last few years. What an idyllic setting for a romantic wedding.

As if she hadn't enough to do, Chrissie decided twenty years ago, to get out of the farm and meet people by teaching English. In France, there is a big demand for English, by adults in work. It is hard for them to admit, but English has overtaken French by miles and companies cannot get far without English nowadays. So Chrissie teaches small groups of adults in their workplace – which could be a widget factory or a luxury hotel. This is besides writing and editing her twenty years' worth of columns which she hopes to publish in book form. There are still groups of farming enthusiasts who come to the farm for visits and a meal and now there is the extended family too.

Is there anything they miss about England? Yes – English pubs and English humour. There are bars in France, but they are places where workmen go on the way home for an *apéro* (*apéritif*) before dinner – you rarely see women in these country bars, and anyway, they are closed by 9.30 pm. There are restaurants, but a restaurant is different from the English country pub. There are discos, usually hidden away in a forest out of town, but these are for the young.

Chrissie thinks the French do take themselves seriously and don't like to laugh at themselves. 'There would never be a Comic Relief Day here', she says. 'A fireman would never dream of shaving his legs, nor would a politician wear a red nose. That's not to say the French don't give to charities - they do. It's just that they don't want to make it a joke.'

Would they ever go back? An emphatic 'No' to this one. 'If you move to France when your children are young and they grow up being French, then you are much more firmly-rooted here.' Furthermore, the cost of property in England is prohibitive after so many years here. Tim has seen Nantwich when visiting relatives and said the old farms in Cheshire had mostly gone to make way for houses for the new rich – the footballers and 'wags'. England isn't for them now, they say.

Chrissie and Tim in their farmhouse kitchen

24 Noel, Noel
December 2010 / January 2011

I am staring out of the windows at the oak and apple trees wearing clouds of mistletoe and thinking I could make a bomb on a Christmas market – it's just unfortunate that I'm in Normandy and not in England. But I assume you are and that you are thinking about all the paraphernalia of Christmas. If you aren't, and haven't started the merry-go-round that is Christmas, you will not be able to ignore it much longer. I did think things would be different in France but increasingly, western commercialism is taking over and making Christmas much the same everywhere in Europe.

Strangely enough, this is not the case for Halloween. Halloween is on the wane here in France whereas in the USA it is so big an occasion that it threatens to eclipse Christmas. I can only think that Halloween, clashes with the weekend of All Saints, when families here in France take flowers to the cemetery to remember their dear departed. Maybe people have worked out that the gravity of the weekend doesn't fit with the silliness of modern Halloween. There is of course the fact that any youngster trick-or-treating at houses in the countryside (and the majority of the population live outside big cities) is likely to have a bite taken out of their backside by some ferocious guard-dog.

Twenty years ago, Christmas decorations outside houses were unknown and now they are as much part of the scenery as the shutters on those very houses. Now, I know the French are supposed to be known for their elegance but believe me, their taste in outdoor decorations in no way enhances their reputation. How is a child to believe in Santa, if Santa can be seen climbing every other chimney? They may not put up these illuminations until the middle of December – rather later than in England now, but they certainly don't bother taking them down until, let's see – ooh, Easter. That's one thing that thankfully has remained true in England – decorations and the tree are taken down and put out of sight on the 6th of January which is the twelfth night. Maybe this has become a superstitious warning of bad luck if you don't, but in that case I wish the French believed more in bad luck. Just how far this Christmas decoration fashion has gone is illustrated by the fact that our village is having an outing – a bus tour of eight villages now renowned for their Christmas illuminations. True, there is going to be a stop off for dinner at a farmhouse which probably will tempt us to go, but still...

Inside, it's a different story in France – just a Christmas tree and a crib, or at least little figurines depicting the Christmas story. While you are visiting, you notice something else missing too – Christmas cards. The French are not quite as into cards for any occasion as we and the Americans are - perhaps because they are more likely to say it with flowers. In any case, any cards they send are in the New Year after January 1st, to friends they rarely see – friends abroad or in another region – and that means fewer than ten.

I'd tried to explain what Christmas cards mean to us last week to our neighbours, in the course of an *apéro*, and they took a long time to grasp that we send around 100 cards, that we have a Christmas card list that is brought out every year, only for dead people to be stricken off the list, before you write them out. This is a two-man job in our house. My husband usually writes the bit in the card and I write the envelopes. It's a mammoth task to send a card to just everyone we think of as dear to us: friends, acquaintances, work colleagues – even somebody at the desk next to you. Warming to my theme as they gazed at me open-mouthed, I explained that you must have a reserve pile of cards in case you receive a card from someone you haven't sent one to, otherwise that person will be mightily offended. You send one to your next-door neighbours when you could instead invite them round for a drink. You even send one to people who you could visit but don't because you don't really like them enough. So in that case, a Christmas card can be a poor consolation for a lack of friendship.

We had the French neighbours in stitches when Eric told them about the relatively new 'round robin' letter in which you tell everyone nothing bad or sad or negative in any way, but everything wonderful with the result that all these round robins are a ridiculous boast about children's talents, intelligence and the parents' madly busy and fulfilled life.

For the French, it's the food that is the most important thing about Christmas. The first meal or *réveillon* is served late on Christmas Eve, traditionally after going to late mass, although not a lot of French people go to church anymore. Turkey is traditional but increasingly, there is also *pâté de foie gras* and oysters. There is no Christmas pudding or cake as we know it but a *bouche de Noel* – a yule log. At this meal the children open their presents so there is none of the early Christmas morning awakening for French parents. The grown-ups exchange presents at New Year – that's why the sales here start well into January, when all the presents have been bought, and not after Christmas. The next day in the afternoon, the whole thing is repeated with a change of menu. Christmas is generally when the family get together and the New Year is when friends get-together for parties.

Party-wise, the people I have taught over the years, in all sorts of businesses, don't seem to go in for the office-party (surprising isn't it, given the flirtatious reputation of French men? Maybe it's just not serious enough for their taste?). So they were rather shocked by my descriptions of the typical office party in England with the shenanigans that are regretted the morning after. It's just a reflection of the fact that Christmas, for the French, is a family time.

It doesn't finish there, though, as on the 6th of January, the feast of the Epiphany, there is yet another meal – the whole village comes to that. It's when they like to eat sauerkraut and a special cake called *La Galette des Rois* (the kings' cake), inside which is *la fève*, a tiny figurine. Whoever finds *la fève* in their gateau is declared king or queen of the feast.

Before Christmas in France, you have the dustmen, the firemen, the postman and even the local police knocking at your door. They have come to give you a calendar for the New Year. This means you are expected to give them a minimum of €10.00 each for the privilege.

What is missing about Christmas in France and what I miss a lot from England, is carol singing, both the organised sort in town centres and door-to-door and Christmas crackers - how do you explain those abysmal jokes and silly hats that are somehow the whole point of granddads at Christmas?

Sarkozy will be speaking to the French nation on New Year's Eve but I doubt that it has the same place in the hearts of French people as does the Queen's speech. We English are probably more cynical than the French most of the year, but at precisely 3 pm on Christmas Day we will all be turning on the telly, replete from the turkey dinner, a glass of our favourite tipple in hand. Now that's solidarity.

Vivienne M. Barker

Vivienne taught French to 'A' level throughout a period when 'twinning' with a French town was a popular extracurricular activity. As a teacher, she was lucky enough to be billeted with different French families each year. Later, she moved to Normandy and lived there for fifteen years.

During this time, Vivienne taught English to French business people in diverse places of work like solicitors' offices, chocolate factories, hotels, casinos and agricultural sites.

This book is a compilation of articles Vivienne wrote for 'Northern Life', a cultural magazine in the North of England. Each chapter examines one aspect of French life in order to appreciate the differences between our two cultures.

If you are thinking of holidaying in France or buying property in France, if you are studying French or merely curious about the French, this book is an excellent introduction to what you are letting yourself in for.

A chapter a day gives food for thought, something to chat over with friends or something to argue about with your French connections.

vivienne.barker@gmail.com